Ebert's Bigger Little Movie Glossary

Ebert's Bigger Little Movie Glossary

A Greatly Expanded and
Much Improved Compendium of
Movie Clichés, Stereotypes,
Obligatory Scenes,
Hackneyed Formulas,
Shopworn Conventions, and
Outdated Archetypes

By Roger Ebert

**Andrews McMeel
Publishing**

Kansas City

Ebert's Bigger Little Movie Glossary copyright © 1999 by Roger Ebert.
All rights reserved. Printed in the United States of America. No part
of this book may be used or reproduced in any manner whatsoever
without written permission except in the case of reprints in the context
of reviews. For information write Andrews McMeel Publishing, an
Andrews McMeel Universal company, 4520 Main Street, Kansas City,
Missouri 64111.

"Mark O'Donnell's Laws of Cartoon Motion" © 1980
by Mark O'Donnell. Reprinted by kind permission.

"A Cynic's Guide to the Language in Film Festival Catalog
Descriptions," © 1998, *Toronto Globe and Mail*

  00 01 02 03 RDH 10 9 8 7 6 5 4 3

www.andrewsmcmeel.com

Library of Congress Cataloging-in-Publication Data

Ebert's bigger little movie glossary : a greatly expanded and much
   improved compendium of movie clichés, stereotypes, obligatory
   scenes, hackneyed formulas, shopworn conventions, and outdated
   archetypes / [edited] by Roger Ebert.
       p. cm.
     ISBN 0-8362-8289-2 (paperback)
       1. Motion pictures–Humor. 2. Clichés in motion pictures.
   I. Ebert, Roger. II. Title: Bigger little movie glossary.
   PN1994.9.E19   1999
   791.43'02'07–dc21   99-11008
                                                                 CIP

Design by Holly Camerlinck
Composition by Kelly & Company, Lee's Summit, Missouri

This book is for
Raven, Emil, and Taylor
Corvo, Emilio, and Piccolino

Contents

Introduction

The birth of the critical impulse comes in different ways to different people, and to some it comes not at all. Reconstructing my own development as a critic, I usually cite Dwight Macdonald's columns in *Esquire* as the key early influence. In the late 1950s and 1960s, *Esquire* was the best magazine in America, and I treated it like a road map to life. Macdonald was pointed, unforgiving, hard to please, and very funny.

But there was, I find, an even earlier influence. That would be *Mad* magazine, which had an almost incalculable effect on America in the 1950s. In the world of bland Eisenhower calm, there were whirlpools of satire: *Mad*, Bob and Ray, Stan Freberg, Lenny Bruce. I was going to the movies once or twice a week, and when I read the *Mad* satires of movies, I learned about clichés, stereotypes, obligatory scenes, standard dialogue, and preposterous plot developments. I began to apply what I learned to the movies I was seeing, and by the time I was in high school, that had become a habit.

Perhaps this *Glossary* grew out of those old issues of *Mad*. Years later, as a film critic for the *Chicago Sun-Times,* I sat down at a typewriter and wrote down twenty or thirty "glossary entries" for a Sunday column. Why? It seemed like a good idea at the time. Recently I've been scanning some of my earliest reviews into digital form, and in re-reading them, I find that I was forever pointing out the ways in which movies followed generic conventions, whether to honor or dishonor them. It seemed to be the way my mind worked.

The first column led to others. When I started publishing annual collections of reviews in 1986, a list of glossary entries appeared in each book. Readers started sending in contributions of their own. In 1991, my reviews and the glossary were picked up by CompuServe, and I was given a section of the ShowBiz Forum. Now a trickle became a flood (nice cliché).

Ebert's Little Movie Glossary was published in 1994, and also appeared in a British edition titled *The Little Book of Hollywood Clichés.* And I received still more submissions; I started using a new one every other week in my column "The Movie Answer Man."

Now here is *Ebert's Bigger Little Movie Glossary.* It's about twice the size of the first edition, although most of the earlier entries have been retained (I would not want to do without the Fruit Cart or the Talking Killer). About two-thirds of the entries are by readers, including some prolific ones. To them, my thanks.

The purpose of the book is to entertain, of course, but perhaps it might also shame filmmakers into avoiding the most shopworn conventions. The Fruit Cart syndrome has actually been satirized in more than one film, and I await the day when the *Glossary* itself is filmed. I imagine an entire film made of clichés, archetypes, and stereotypes; then I reflect that such a movie is released more or less weekly.

Will there be a third edition someday? Who knows? Contributions still flow in. You can mail them to me at the *Sun-Times,* 401 N. Wabash, Chicago 60610. Or E-mail me at 74774.2267@compuserve.com. New entries appear in the Answer Man column, which is syndicated to 305 papers and appears on-line on CompuServe, or at www.sun-times.com/ebert.

As this book went to press, I lost my friend and colleague Gene Siskel, who supplied some of these entries, and coined Siskel's Test: "Is this movie as interesting as a documentary of the same actors having lunch?" That's a question every filmmaker would be wise to ask before embarking on a new project.

ROGER EBERT

Academy Mandate. The feeling by Oscar winners that an award for their film work is a validation of their personal beliefs. Examples: Vanessa Redgrave's "Zionist hoodlum" speech; Oliver Stone's insistence that his awards for *Platoon* were an anti–Vietnam War statement by the Academy; Richard Attenborough's accepting the Oscar for *Gandhi* the movie on behalf of Gandhi the man; James Cameron asking for a moment of silence for the *Titanic* victims, etc.

MERWYN GROTE, *St. Louis*

Accentuating Evil. The xenophobic and frequently anglophobic practice of defining villains by their distinctive accents, from twangy southern sheriffs to meticulously dictioned elitist snobs to wheezing Teutonic mad scientists. The hiring of British actors to play accented villains is particularly prevalent. Examples: Alec Guinness in *Hitler: The Last Ten Days,* Laurence Olivier in *Marathon Man,* Peter Sellers in *Dr. Strangelove,* Jeremy Irons in *Reversal of Fortune, The Lion King, Die Hard 3*, etc.

MERWYN GROTE, *St. Louis*

Acquariamcam. Underwater action scenes, even in the dirty waters of major ports, are always crystal clear, pristine, and well lit. Although characters are submerged longer than it would take me to get a popcorn refill, upon surfacing they start talking immediately.

JIM CAREY, *New Lenox, Ill.*

Actress Inferior Position. In movie sex scenes, which are usually directed by men, the POV at the moment of

Acquariamcam

climax is almost always the man's, so that we see the actress, not the actor, losing control.

GENE SISKEL

AC-WAT-NOBI Movie. A Cop with a Theory No One Believes In.

ROBERT TARRY GROUCHY, *University of Calgary*

Against All Odds Rule. In an apparently fatal situation from which there is no possible hope of survival, it is certain the characters will survive. In a situation where there is any apparent chance of survival, there will be at least some deaths.

R. R. KUNZ

The Agent Did It! In any film involving an unknown killer, if a moderately well-known actor is given costar billing yet only appears for, say, five minutes in the first hour and a half, he or she is almost guaranteed to be revealed at the climax as the murderer, complete with flamboyant mad scene leading up to a spectacular death.

MICHAEL SCHLESINGER, *Culver City, Calif.*

Aging Blood Syndrome. Tendency of movie blood to look more and more like gushes of slightly crimson motor oil every year (as in all nineties horror and action movies), as opposed to anything possibly resembling real blood (as in *The Wild Bunch*).

LUKAS KENDALL, *Martha's Vineyard, Mass.*

"Ain't Nobody Here but Us Chickens." Whenever someone is alone at home at night and they hear a sound in the house and ask aloud, "(Name), is that you?" it *never* is.

JAMES PORTANOVA

Airline Flight Rules. Movie characters travel only first class. They are never seated near crying babies. All flights are full, but they are always able to walk right on and take their seats without waiting behind someone cramming a suitcase into an overhead rack. Although other passengers on the flight may recline their seats, the main characters can only be seated in the full upright position, because if they reclined the result would be an unattractive camera angle up their nostrils.

JAMES FUHRMAN, *West Hollywood, Calif.*

Air Vent Escape Route. If the hero is imprisoned in a building owned by the villains, there will inevitably be an air vent cover that is not screwed in and is easily removed. The passageway will be large enough to accommodate any size person. The escape route will pass over the room where the bad guys are discussing the details of their diabolical plan, which the hero will now be able to foil.

DONA KIGHT, *Chicago*

Alan Alda Rule. Any character in a murder mystery who is excessively helpful to the main character invariably turns out to be the killer (if he or she isn't dead by the second reel). Named for Alda because he's done it at least twice.

ROB MATSUSHITA, *Madison, Wis.*

Alarm Clock Rule. If an electric clock is given a close-up, it will be either twenty-nine minutes past the hour, or one minute to the hour. The time will progress one minute, waking up the hero with a song that is important to the plot.

RHYS SOUTHAN, *Richardson, Tex.*

Alien Berlitz Communication Rule (ABC Rule). Movie aliens are able to learn the local language (English, French, Japanese, etc.) in an amazingly short time. Frequently this includes the ability to reproduce recognizable Earth-like accents. See also "Universal Translator."

RICHARD ROHRDANZ, *West Kennebunk, Maine*

Ali MacGraw's Disease. Movie illness in which only symptom is that the sufferer grows more beautiful as death approaches.

R. E.

All-Seeing Camera. The remarkable ability of a stationary surveillance camera or news camera operated by a lone cameraman to film or video an incident from several different angles and distances all at once. When played back, the resulting film or videotape exactly duplicates the original point of view of the audience, right down to the sequence of the montage. See *Enemy of the State*, etc.

MERWYN GROTE, *St. Louis*

All the News That's Scripted, We Print. All media coverage depicted in a movie will prominently feature the

Animal Kingdom, Sights and Sound Of

main character, no matter how incidental his or her involvement is to the big story. His picture makes Page One, and CNN thoroughly documents his simple presence in a crowd. See *Godzilla,* in which TV news reports pass up footage of a giant rampaging lizard in favor of shots of Matthew Broderick carrying his luggage, digging a hole, etc.

JAMES ARNALL, St. Louis

Angelic Bicyclist. Whenever movie characters are seen blissfully riding their bicycles with eyes closed and arms outstretched like angel's wings, there is a strong likelihood that they are about to collide with a massive object and be killed.

JEFF SHANNON, Seattle

Angel Limited-Involvement Rule. Modern movie angels mostly seem to visit Earth in order to smoke cigarettes, eat pizza, and show what regular Joes they are. Although famine, war, disease, and higher prices torment the globe, they solve such problems as a guy who has stopped dating because he's lost his faith in women.

R. E.

Animal Kingdom, Sights and Sound Of. (1) In at least one scene in any movie about the "jungle"–no matter where in the world–the sound track must feature the demented call *("who-who-who-ah-ah-ah-ah-HA-HA")* of an Australian kookaburra (the "Laughing Jackass Bird"). (2) Except when dogs pee on someone's foot for comic effect, animals on film never micturate or defecate. (3) Before 1970, any predatory mammal–wildcat, wolf, or bear–was vicious and bad, deserving to be shot by the good guy. Now they've become noble and powerful—and somehow less carnivorous; perhaps they have discovered tofu.

STEVE W. ZACK, *Nedding, Calif.*

Anti-Anti-Auto Theft Device. Any actor can start any car by pulling any two wires from under the dash and touching them together to make them spark. This not only starts the car but it also defeats the steering column's locking mechanism.

COLOM KEATING, *Santa Monica, Calif.*

Antiheroine Skin Rule. In a Horny Teenager Movie, the "bad girl" who is the object of the hero's desire will always expose more flesh than the girl whom he ends up with at the end of the film, despite equal sexual activity. If the "good girl" is shown topless in a love scene, it must be accompanied by slow music. In a Dead Teenager Movie, the girl who exposes the least skin is inevitably the only survivor.

JIM O'BRIEN

Antiques of Death. Straight razors, ice picks, paperweights, fireplace pokers, meat cleavers, crowbars, dueling pistols, ceremonial daggers, swords, sabers, battle-axes, giant marble ashtrays, and other archaic, clichéd weapons of mayhem that always seem to be handy for movie murders, even though few homes might actually have any such antiques readily available for an impromptu killing.

MERWYN GROTE, *St. Louis*

Archivist Killer Syndrome. Many serial killers could also find employment as the authors of double acrostics and conundrums. In searching for such killers, hero detectives invariably find an abandoned apartment with newspaper clippings and photos on the wall showing the killer's (a) victims, (b) pursuer, (c) next victim, and (d) a message to his pursuers. See *In the Line of Fire, Seven.*

DAVID T. G. RICHES, *Etobicoke, Ontario*

Ark Movie

Ark Movie. Dependable genre in which a mixed bag of characters is trapped on a colorful mode of transportation. Examples: *Airport* (airplane), *The Poseidon Adventure* (ocean liner), *Marooned* (space satellite), *The Cassandra Crossing* (train), *Aliens* (outer space), *The Hindenberg* (dirigible), *The Taking of Pelham One Two Three* (subway train), *Abyss* (undersea station), and of course the best of them all, *Stagecoach*.

R. E.

Ashes to Lashes. In any scene involving the scattering of ashes, the ashes will blow back into the faces of the mourners. See *The Big Lebowski*.

R. E.

Asian Grandfather Rule (Yan's Law). All elderly Asians in movies speak in aphorisms like Sydney Toler in the old Charlie Chan movies.

BILL BECWAR, *Wauwatosa, Wis.*

Asian Woman Rule. Any Asian woman with a greater than incidental part in a movie always falls in love with the hero, no matter how big a slob he seems to her (or any other) culture.

BILL BECWAR, *Wauwatosa, Wis.*

"As Long as You're Up, Get Me a 2 × 4." When a fight in a bar breaks out, nearly everyone in the place begins fighting, spontaneously and without cause—even with people they have been sitting next to for some time.

JIM SIMON, *Villa Park, Calif.*

Auto Audio Rule. The sound a vehicle makes in a movie chase scene will in no way correspond to any sound made by same vehicle in real life (tires squealing on dirt or around corners at low speed, etc.).

EDWARD SAVIO, *San Francisco*

"As Long as You're Up, Get Me a 2 × 4."

Auto Autopilot Exemption. An actor required to deliver key dialogue while driving a car is allowed to take his or her eyes off the road and maintain steady eye contact with the front-seat passenger for up to five seconds without being subject to real-life consequences like rear-ending a cement mixer or taking out pedestrians.

DAVID MAYEROVITCH, *Toronto*

Autobiographical Cameo Perk. If a flattering movie is made about a person who is still alive, watch for that person to make a fleeting cameo in the film, a perk for relinquishing the rights to his existence. Examples: Melvin Dumar selling sandwiches in *Melvin and Howard,* Jim Garrison playing Earl Warren in *JFK,* Blaze Starr as a stripper in *Blaze,* or Jim Lovell playing an admiral in *Apollo 13.* (This is parodied in *Pee-Wee's Big Adventure* when Pee-Wee Herman makes a cameo appearance in the movie-within-the movie.)

MERWYN GROTE, *St. Louis*

Auto Death Knell. If a character dies in a car crash, he will do so in a way that causes the horn to blare continuously.

JOHN SHANNON, *Oceanside, Calif.*

Automatically Arriving Automobiles. Whenever cars in a chase go through a four-way junction, unrelated cars must appear from each direction and skid into the center. These cars may either stop unharmed or crash into each other in the center, upon which all the drivers will get out and shake fists at each other. No cars actually involved in the chase are ever involved in the crash.

STEPHEN ROWLEY, *Melbourne, Australia*

Automatic Bike Bell. Any bicycle passing through the frame will be accompanied by the ring of a bike bell on the sound track.

R. E.

Automatic Customer Bell. All establishing shots of small town Main Streets are inevitably accompanied by the sound of a bell ringing as a customer opens a door.

R. E.

Automatic Miss Syndrome. In every movie in which the hero or heroine is fleeing from automatic weapons fire, the bullets will strike either in front or behind or, in a more aesthetically pleasing pattern, in parallel rows on either side.

KIM ROTZOLL, *Urbana, Ill.*

Automatic Vest Display. A character who has mysteriously survived being shot at point-blank range always immediately unbuttons his shirt to reveal his bulletproof vest, usually only to himself.

R. E.

Backseater Mortality Phenomenon. Whenever the hero is the pilot of a warplane that has a crew of two or more, any crewman that is not a pilot is marked for death. See *Top Gun, Flight of the Intruder, Enemy Mine, By Dawn's Early Light,* and *The Empire Strikes Back.*

JEFF CROSS, *Marblehead, Mass.*

Back Seat Inviso-Syndrome. Film characters are invariably unable to see a person crouched in the back seat of a car (even a convertible) when, in the real world, it is an impossible place for a person to hide.

ERIC SKOVAN, *Poughkeepsie, N.Y.*

Bad Guy Credentials Demo. In any movie where the villain is a really, really bad guy, whose dysfunction and malice transcend that of the ordinary evildoer, he establishes that fact early in the film by coldly killing one of his own men. See Darth Vader, many Bond villains, Russian Mafia leader in *The Jackal,* etc.

DIRK KNEMEYER, *Bowling Green, Ohio*

Baked Potato People

Bad Movie Rental Warning Rule. If a rental movie box has a warning such as "If scenes of graphic horror offend you, do not rent this film!"–do not rent this film.

Sam Waas, Houston

Bad Smoker Rule. In any cop movie made since the mid-seventies, the bad guys smoke, while the good guy is trying to quit.

R. E.

Baguette Envy. In every scene which includes a person carrying a bag of groceries, the bag will invariably contain a long, skinny, French baguette loaf, and exactly 8.5 inches of it will be exposed.

MICHAEL J. PILLING, *Maple Ridge, B.C., Canada*

Baked Potato People. The nice, good, sweet little people who form a chorus in the hero's background, especially during any movie set in a mental home (cf. *The Dream Team, Crazy People*). The lesson is always the same: It's the real world that's crazy, and the crazy people who speak real truth. (Inspired by a sign seen by Billy Baxter of New York City on a baked potato in a steak house: "I've been tubbed, I've been rubbed, I've been scrubbed. I'm lovable, huggable, and eatable!")

R. E.

Balloon Rule. Good movies rarely contain a hot-air balloon. Most egregious use of a hot-air balloon: *Men Don't Leave,* where the heroine is cured of clinical depression by a ride in one. (Readers keep writing in with exceptions to this rule, including *Witness,* but the general principle still applies.)

R. E.

Balls of Steel Rule. Bad guys who suffer a blow to the groin are down for the count, just like in real life. Good guys shrug it off and are back in action within seconds. See, in particular, *Total Recall,* in which Sharon Stone kicks Schwarzenegger in the groin a half-dozen times within a matter of minutes. Arnold only grits his teeth.

JOHN SNELL

Balloon Rule

Barber's Itch Rule. Major stars in a film about army recruits going through basic training will never have their head shaved completely. Their hair will merely be short (for example, Bill Murray and Harold Ramis in *Stripes,* Richard Gere in *An Officer and a Gentleman*). Likewise, a star entering prison will only have a tasteful trim (Robert Redford in *Brubaker*).

Jon Niccum, *Kansas City, Mo.*

Barroom Bum Slide. Most bar fights in the movies end with the loser being pushed so hard he slides halfway down the bar. In real life, this is impossible.

Douglas W. Topham, *Woodland Hills, Calif.*

Bartender Establishing Shot. All movie bartenders, when first seen, are wiping the inside of a glass with a rag.

David W. Smith, *Westminister, Calif.*

"Based on a true story." Hollywood shorthand, meaning: Depressing, morbid, downbeat, including scenes so shocking or lascivious that no producer would include them in a movie unless he could excuse himself by saying these things actually happened.

Rich Elias, *Delaware, Ohio*

Bathroom Rule. No one ever goes into a movie toilet to perform a natural function. Instead characters use the bathroom to take illegal drugs, commit suicide, have sex, smoke, get killed, exchange money, or sneak out through the bathroom window.

Eugene Accardo, *Brooklyn, N.Y.*

17

"Because It's Called Sound Effects" Rule. In real life, when someone hangs up the phone on you, you hear a click and then silence (about thirty seconds of dead air before an obnoxious tone). In the movies, when someone hangs up at the other end, you get a new dial tone immediately.

JOHN FARMER, *Manhattan Beach, Calif.*

Because They Are There. The top ten lines you can always count on in a mountain-climbing movie: (1) "We have to move fast. We've started late in the season. But if we leave behind the oxygen and most of our equipment and travel light, we can get up there and back before the winter storms." (2) "I know they're still alive." (3) "Leave me here. I can't walk. My legs are broken. By yourself, you have a chance." (4) "Just let me do this one last climb. Then I'll settle down with you and the baby." (5) "Tell them they'll get an extra fifty rupees a day, at the end, if they complete this part of the march." (6) "Sahib! The fresh snow has covered up the crevices! The men say they will go no further today!" (7) "Every previous expedition along this route has had trouble with the porters." (8) "I'd trust him on the other end of my rope." (9) "Take me along. You know I'm a better climber than those guys." (10) "Because it's there."

R. E.

Beep Bleep. The sneaky trick of inserting the honk of a car horn onto the sound track to cover an obscene word or phrase. Whistles, bells, animal noises, and claps of thunder are also used. Sometimes used to turn an R-rated film

Because They Are There

into a PG-13, but more frequently used to clean up the TV version. See also "Crap Gap" and "Inanity Profanity."

MERWYN GROTE, *St. Louis*

Beeping Rule. In movies where cops, reporters, hackers, and others are using a computer to locate a suspect or special file, the successful retrieval of said subject is heralded with dramatic beeps, flashing messages, and other electronic indications that "something important has been found." The only time an ordinary computer ever beeps is when it refuses to carry out a command.

JAMES MOORE, *San Jose, Calif.*

Beginning, The. Word used in the titles of sequels to movies in which everyone was killed at the end of the original movie, making an ordinary sequel impossible. Explains to knowledgeable filmgoers that the movie will concern, for example, what happened in the Amityville house before the Lutzes moved in. Other examples: The First Chapter, The Early Days, etc.

R. E.

Benevolent Blurbster. A week before a movie opens, all the reviews seem to be ecstatic. Sunday papers and advance TV ads are filled with shouts of unqualified praise, usually attributed to unfamiliar critics from obscure outlets. These "critics" exist primarily for the purpose of supplying such advance quotes, which they are happy to do for the thrill of seeing their names in print. Often they do not even write an actual review, but compose only the blurbs, which they fax or telephone to grateful publicists.

Wise moviegoers wait until quotes from real critics from respected sources start appearing in the ads.

R. E.

Bergman-Allen Hypothesis. Ingmar Bergman regards existential depression as a flaw in the universe. For Woody Allen, it's just hereditary.

RICH ELIAS, Delaware, Ohio

Best Play of the Game Rule. Every bad sports movie ends with the hero making an extraordinary catch/play/hit in slow motion to win the game at the final gun/bell/buzzer.

WEBSTER WATNIK

"Betcha Can't Name That Tune" Ploy. Almost all movie pianists, such as Clint Eastwood in *In the Line of Fire*, are perfectly happy playing nothing but chords. By never straying anywhere near a recognizable melody, they avoid paying royalties.

EMO PHILLIPS, Chicago

***Betsy* Syndrome.** Identifying an actor in print by his or her latest film, regardless of how weak it was. Inspired by a newspaper article that appeared toward the end of Sir Lawrence Olivier's career, referring to him as "Lawrence *(The Betsy)* Olivier."

BRIAN JONES

Big Gun Recoil Rule. Any large gun must fire with such force that it causes the barrel or some other part of the gun to recoil. In defiance of the laws of physics, this rule applies even to laser cannons in sci-fi movies. See *Star Trek V, Star Wars* trilogy.

JEFF CROSS, *Marblehead, Mass.*

Big Lie, The. Refers to all scenes where bad guy paints a beautiful picture and then adds a version of, "One more thing, Benny. I Lied."

MIKE SHEEHAN

Big Name Poster Rule. When the entire trailer or poster for a movie consists of the names of the two stars, as in STALLONE-STONE or WESLEY-WOODY, this suggests that getting those two names represents most of the film's budget, and that finding a script was a lower priority.

MARK MCDERMOTT, *Park Forest, Ill.*

Big Nod, The. Comes after the Last Word. After a character is fatally wounded, first he lies motionless and recites an incredibly meaningful statement. Then his head nods to one side.

REX E. RUSSO

Big Wet Dog Shakedown. All wet dogs shake themselves dry only while standing next to well-dressed movie characters.

STEVE WIDEMAN

Bilingual Nazi Officer Rule. Nazi officers always speak English when talking to each other, even though Nazi sergeants can be heard in the background barking orders in German.

TIM BENTON, *Huntsville, Ala.*

Birthin' Rule. Any character more than seven months pregnant will give birth by the end of the film, usually in an unusual place, such as an elevator, a cemetery, or the back seat of a car in a traffic jam. The baby is always delivered by someone squeamish and inexperienced who will discover the miracle of life and get the baby named after him or her.

LISA MARTIN, *Toronto*

Black Rock Rule. When a movie starts with the hero arriving in a small town to look up a long lost friend or relative, the person is almost certainly already dead and half the town is in on it. Named for *Bad Day at Black Rock*.

JOE DiCOSTANZO, *New York City*

Blockbuster–Brady Bill Postulate. Since at least one out of every three movie covers at the average video store shows someone holding a gun, you should probably wait at least five business days before renting them.

JEFFREY R. FIELD, *Kansas City*

Bloody Fingertip Rule. If a character sees anything looking like blood, he must put his finger in it and hold it up before realizing that it is blood. Corollary: If the substance is not blood, the character must smell it or taste it before realizing what it is.

GERALD FITZGERALD, *Dallas*

Body Switch Movie. The brain of one character somehow finds itself in the body of another. Requires actors to confront an actor's nightmare, i.e., acting as if they were another actor.

R. E.

Bogeyman Shot. Unaware victim is shot in close-up looking toward the camera, while a huge lopsided space is left vacant for the monster/killer to appear in.

PAUL S. WOOLEY, *Portland, Oreg.*

Bomb Defusion Rule. No bomb can be defused if it is more than ten seconds away from detonation.

GERALD FITZGERALD, *Dallas*

Boob Tube. There is never anything worth watching on TV in the movies.

JERRY RITCEY

Boom-Boom Rule. Whenever a building or a car explodes, the explosion will be repeated in its entirety from several different camera angles.

SAM CARLSON, *Duluth, Minn.*

Born in the USA. Any movie set in an unnamed U.S. city will be revealed by the credits to have been filmed in Toronto or Vancouver.

R. R. KUNZ

Box Rule. Beware movies advertised with a row of little boxes across the bottom, each one showing the face of a different international star and the name of a character (e.g., "Curt Jurgens as the Commandant"). Also, most films made from Agatha Christie novels.

R. E.

Boy-Meets-Girl Rules. If two characters have a Meet Cute, they'll be together by the end of the movie. If they have an antagonistic meet, they'll be together by the middle of the movie.

BARBARA BRIDGES, *Los Angeles*

Brando Acceptability Yardstick. After Marlon Brando did *Superman* strictly for the money, he cleared the way for Gene Hackman, Jack Nicholson, Faye Dunaway, Warren Beatty, Dustin Hoffman, Al Pacino, and others to take big bucks to appear in silly comic book roles. (Illustrated in Blake Edward's *S.O.B.* when Julie Andrews is asked to do a nude scene because Liv Ullman has done one.)

MERWYN GROTE, *St. Louis*

Brass Ring Rule. Any time you overhear incidental dialogue from minor characters about some impossible feat, occasionally attempted but never achieved, someone, usually the hero, will accomplish the feat within the last ten minutes of the movie.

BRANNON MOORE, *Seattle*

Breaking Bad News: Anyone holding a vase or other glass object will drop that object upon hearing bad news. Usually the object will fall and shatter in slow motion, typically from multiple angles.

TERRY MCMANUS, *Chicago*

Breathing Corpse Syndrome. No one in the movies or on television has ever looked convincingly dead, a condition much harder to fake than an orgasm.

PROF. TERRY EAGLETON, *Oxford University, England*

25

Breaking Bad News

Brick Wall Paradox. If a character, while swinging on a rope in an affluent suburb, slams face-first into a brick wall, that character never experiences any injuries other than moaning and sliding off of the wall. See *Home Alone, Cops and Robbersons.*

ROD AHLBRANDT, Laramie, Wyo.

British Roman Rule. All leaders of the Roman Empire have British accents. Why don't filmmakers want Romans to at least have Italian accents?

EUGENE ACCARDO, Brooklyn

Broken Compass Principle. In New York City chase scenes, cars are able to turn off of avenues onto other avenues. This is impossible, since the avenues are parallel.

DAVID BURD, East Stroudsburg, Pa.

Brotman's Law. "If nothing has happened by the end of the first reel, nothing is going to happen." (Decreed by Chicago movie exhibitor Oscar Brotman.)

R. E.

Buddy-Brother Road Film. Three-way combo of buddy movie, road movie, and brothers who learn to love each other. See *Coupe de Ville, Rain Man, The Wizard.*

JOHN WECKMUELLER, Menomonie, Wis.

Bud "The Stud" Drumplehoff's Law. Dramatic films don't have crew member nicknames in the credits. Comedies do.

GREG BROWN, Chicago

Bullet Velocity Rule. In action movies, the speed of a bullet is slowed down enough so that our hero can jump out of the way. In sci-fi movies, the speed of light (lasers/phasers/blasters) is slowed down enough so that the hero/ship can jump/move out of the way and the audience can see the beam moving. The actual formula is: Hollywood Bullet Speed = (Real Bullet Speed) / (Importance of Character), where the more important a character is, the higher the number.

DAVE EDSON, *Eugene, Oreg.*

Bullitt Rule. Any car chase in San Francisco will be downhill, even though the most likely places from which someone would flee are all downtown, at the bottom of all of the hills.

NEIL MILSTED, *Chicago*

***Bullitt* Shift.** Cars in high-speed chases can shift through more gears than they have. See *Bullitt,* where Steve McQueen's car upshifts more than sixteen times.

EDWARD SAVIO, *San Francisco*

Bumbling Night Watchman. Any scene involving the good guy burgling an office at night will inevitably include a semicompetent night watchman, whose sole purpose is to inject an element of danger into an otherwise boring event. Actions performed by the watchman usually include shining a flashlight through the window, rattling doorknobs, watching security monitors, etc., all done in a manner that allows the good guy to continue undetected until just after he discovers the needed information or object. He will then flee the scene with the watchman in pursuit.

RICK NEWBY, *College Place, Wash.*

Bun and Spectacles Rule. Any woman who appears in a movie with her hair in a tight bun and wearing glasses (usually large, thick round ones) will inevitably turn out to be the beautiful heroine. She will magically acquire perfect vision and a sexy wardrobe.

TOM DRANE

Bureau of Lame and Anemic Name Changes (BLANC). Supersecret Hollywood Agency specializing in changing unusual and clever film titles into titles that are banal and uncommercial. Samples: *Cop Gives Waitress $2 Million Tip* became *It Could Happen to You; Sexual Perversity in Chicago* became *About Last Night . . . ; Stab* became *Still of the Night; Cloak and Diapers* became *Undercover Blues; Rocket Boys* became *October Sky,* etc.

MERWYN GROTE, *St. Louis*

But Is It Today's? In a time travel movie, the hero finds out the date by picking up a newspaper in a trash can.

STEVEN SOUZA, *Honolulu, Hawaii*

But They Didn't Count on . . . One Man. In trailers for action movies, this ominous voice-over announces a plot in which the hero single-handedly foils the plans of a band of terrorists or master criminals in spectacular and bloody fashion. See *Die Hard.*

CHRIS GALVIN, *Columbus, Ohio*

But Is It Today's?

Caine-Hackman Theory. Every day of the week, twenty-four hours a day, it is possible to find a movie somewhere on cable TV starring either Michael Caine or Gene Hackman.

> *Cited in the screenplay for* PCU,
> *by* ADAM LEFF *and* ZAK PENN.

Camel, Slow-Moving. All camels in Middle Eastern thrillers are crossing the road for the sole purpose of slowing down a pursuit vehicle.

> R. E.

Camouflage Ramp Certainty Principle. During chase scenes, at least one car will hurtle over a vehicle ramp badly disguised as a normal part of the urban landscape. After flying into the air, the car will usually either strike something and implausibly explode (bad guys) or preposterously survive a landing which should rip the car's suspension to shreds (good guys).

> DOUGLAS M. GARROU, *Seattle*

***Cape Fear* Syndrome.** Derangement that causes heroines, upon learning they are in great danger, to go immediately to an isolated cabin (houseboat, sailboat in the harbor, farm) alone, knowing that no one, especially their friends, will be able to find them.

> CHARLES BOOS, *Evanston, Ill.*

Caring Blanket Tuck-In. Effective in conveying the soft heart of an otherwise unappealing character (e.g., James Woods in *Cop*). Also used in scenes involving the hero,

Caring Blanket Tuck-in

usually as a set-up for a scene in which tucked-in child suddenly finds itself in great danger (e.g., Glenn Ford in *The Big Heat*).

TONY WHITEHOUSE, Verbier, Switzerland

Carl Owens Rooftop Spacer. Any male can accurately predict his ability to jump from one rooftop to another. Women jump and end up hanging from their fingernails and being yanked to safety by the guy who jumped seconds before.

BARAK AND ELIZABETH MOORE, Jerusalem, Israel

Carphand Tunnel Syndrome. In the movies, hackers who type for upward of ten hours a day are unable to put text on their screens any faster than the average second-grader can read along.

ANDY IHNATKO, Westwood, Mass.

Cartop Chases. When there is a foot chase in traffic, the hero will inevitably jump up on top of a car that is stuck in traffic, and leap from car to car, even though it would be faster and safer to stay on the ground (e.g., George Clooney in *The Peacemaker*).

NEIL GABRIELE, New York, N.Y.

Casting Is Destiny. Many Hollywood movies are shaped more by what the audience expects from their stars than by what their writers put into their scripts.

RICH ELIAS, Delaware, Ohio

Cat Sneeze Effect. In movies, when "silenced" guns are fired, they always make the same sound, resembling a cat sneezing. This is nothing like what any gun, silenced or otherwise, sounds like in real life. Also, no matter how big a gun freak a character is, he always refers to these guns as "silenced." Gun experts in real life call them "suppressed."

RAPHAEL CARTER, *Tempe, Ariz.*

Cemetery Weather. Cemeteries generate their own weather. In a surprisingly large number of scenes at cemeteries, particularly if a funeral is in progress, it is raining—and not just sprinkles, but biblical downpours.

G. W. ROLES, *Washington, D.C.*

Centered Passenger Rule. When there is one passenger in the back seat of a car, he always sits right in the middle, to be more easily seen by the camera.

R. E.

Centerfold Folly. With the exception of Marilyn Monroe, no actress who has appeared nude in *Playboy* to advance her acting career has ever actually advanced her acting career.

MERWYN GROTE, *St. Louis*

Chain-Link Fence Rule. Every alley that the police chase a criminal down ends in a chain-link fence that the criminal climbs.

KENNETH C. PARKES

Chamber Music. Hollywood cops in low-budget movies always show their intention to finally confront the villain by withdrawing their pistols and chambering a round. Since a cop is always supposed to be ready to fire his gun if needed, why do they carry them unchambered? Because it looks cool to stick in a round.

DAWSON RAMBO, *Tucson, Ariz.*

Chase-and-Crash Scenes. Replaces the third act or any other form of plot resolution in the modern thriller. After the hero has left dozens of burning cars and trucks behind him, we never see emergency vehicles responding to the carnage. Despite working under a Wrongheaded Commanding Officer, (q.v.), the hero cop is never called on the carpet because yesterday he drove his squad car through the walls of several warehouses.

R. E.

Checker Cab Magnetism. Any character who calls for a cab in a New York movie will be picked up by an old-fashioned Checker cab, although they have not been manufactured in years and, at last count, there were only four still on the streets.

AMY CASH, *Elmont, N.Y.*

Checkmate Reflex. To quickly establish the hero (or villain) as a true (but erratic) genius, he will play a game of chess early in the movie, and quickly trash his opponent with a surprise mate-in-one (e.g., Jeff Goldblum in *Independence Day*).

IVAR LABERG, *Oslo, Norway*

Checkmate Reflex

Child of Sorrow Syndrome. When the hero, regretting the choices he's made in life, returns home in defeat, his bitter self-indictment will be interrupted by his wife, who will say, "I'm having a baby." See *Mr. Holland's Opus, It's a Wonderful Life*, etc.

JIM BECKERMAN, The Record, Hackensack, N.J.

Child Safety Rule. In any monster movie or disaster film, any child under the age of thirteen must survive. In rare instances where a child is killed, the death may not be shown directly.

GERALD FITZGERALD, Dallas, Tex.

Chinese Chase Rule. In any Asian city, or any city with a Chinatown, all chase scenes happen to occur on Chinese New Year, and lead directly through a parade.

NEIL MILSTED, Chicago

Chinese Takeaway. If any American action film of the last decade contains a particularly inventive stunt, there's a better-than-even chance it was swiped from a Hong Kong action film the director recently saw on video.

MICHAEL SCHLESINGER, VP for Acquisitions and Repertory Sales, Sony Pictures, Culver City, Calif.

Chirping Computer Syndrome. Computers in movies always make little chirping sounds when characters hit the screen. Computers and terminals haven't made noises like this since the days of the teletype.

FRED CANTWELL, Ewing, N.J.

Classic Car Rule

Cinematic Business Pathology Syndrome (CBPS).
Affliction that causes sociopathic or criminal behavior by
officers of a corporation. Malady is characterized by several
symptoms. Look for: (1) company located in a run-down
building with a shiny new sign; (2) headquarters in a coldly
contemporary building on a corporate campus devoid of
people; (3) company sign is plain, rectangular, and flat,
with unimaginative artwork; (4) company name includes
words like "amalgamated," "consolidated," "-dyne," "-tron,"
or "chem"; (5) company name includes word "enterprises"
following the name of a man who is bald, is fat, or smokes
a cigar; (6) company premises are dilapidated while company's owner rides in chauffeured limo.

PAUL A. LEE, *Germantown, Wis.*

Cinematic Ear Drum Phenomenon. When movie heroes
get blown out of windows, across streets, into trees, etc.,
they can still hear just fine. In real life, instead of dialogue
like "I'll be back," explosion survivors would be saying,
"What? What? Speak up! I can't hear you!"

DON HOWARD, *San Jose, Calif.*

Citizen's Band Unbound. When two people in the movies
talk over CB or walkie-talkies, they often interrupt each
other in the middle of a sentence, as if they were talking
on a telephone. This is impossible because the sets receive on the same frequency they broadcast on. See the
Die Hard movies.

STEPHEN FOOTE, *Barnesboro, Pa.*

Classic Car Rule. Whenever a beautiful classic car–
usually the prized possession of an unsympathetic father–

is introduced at the beginning of a film, that car will be wrecked by the end of it. See *Risky Business, Ferris Bueller's Day Off, Coupe de Ville,* etc.

R. E.

Cleanliness Is Next to Sexiness. Female characters never bathe or shower except in connection with sex, violence, or implied lesbianism.

R. E.

Clean Up Movie. A motley crew of misfits can't get their act together until a new teacher/coach/nun comes along and straightens them out. Suddenly, they're the best class/team/choir around. Examples: *Summer School, Sister Act* (both parts), *Mr. Baseball, Kindergarten Cop,* etc.

STEVE MYCYNEK, Des Plaines, Ill.

Cleopatra in the Commissary Phenomenon. In any movie about the movies, in any scene shot on a studio back lot, countless extras walk around in outrageous period costumes that haven't been used in years, and recognizable historical figures like Cleopatra, Lincoln, and Napoleon are often seen lined up at the catering line for lunch. (E.g., the two Redcoats in *Get Shorty.*)

GREG BROWN, Chicago

Clichéphobia. Condition afflicting people raised on movies. Symptoms arise when real life situations echo movie clichés, and sufferers must take action to avoid what would be the inevitable denouement in a movie. For example: After saying, "Hey, this is the most perfect day of my life," the clichéphobic realizes that such a statement will mean he's dead before the end of the reel. Or, when a last-minute seat unexpectedly opens up on a fully booked airline flight, the clichéphobic will become convinced that this means the plane is doomed to crash.

MICHAEL MATES and KATHERINE APPLEGATE, *Sarasota, Fla.*

CLIDVIC (Climb from Despair to Victory). Formula for *Rocky* and all the *Rocky* rip-offs. Breaks plot into three parts: (1) defeat and despair; (2) rigorous training, usually shown in the form of would-be MTV videos; (3) victory, preferably ending in freeze-frame of triumphant hero.

R. E.

Climbing Villain. Villains being chased at the end of a movie inevitably disregard all common sense and begin climbing up something—a staircase, a church tower, a mountain—thereby trapping themselves at the top.

TONY WHITEHOUSE, *Verbier, Switzerland*

Clint Howard Scene. In any Ron Howard movie, the scene where his brother, Clint, makes one of his rare acting appearances (in *Backdraft* as the medical examiner, in *Far and Away* as the sweat shop foreman, etc.).

DAWSON E. RAMBO, *Pelham Manor, N.Y.*

Clothes Make the Impostor. Whenever a hit man has to kill someone in a guarded hospital room, he will duck into a linen closet, emerge wearing a lab coat and carrying a clipboard, and walk around the hospital as if invisible. None of the other doctors or nurses will notice that this guy has never worked there before.

MICHAEL FURL, *Kankakee, Ill.*

Clunky Exposition Complex. Fills in vast amounts of background through awkward dialogue. ("You know Betty, we've been married now for five years, and you work in the bean canning factory. I of course have been farming now for all of my life, but despite that, we're still pretty good detectives. I'm sure you remember the assassination of the president of the 4H Club.")

SUZANNE BOOS, *Evanston, Ill.*

Cocking Principle. When a weaker character is holding a gun on a stronger character who doesn't believe the threat, the weaker character merely has to cock the gun, and the stronger character will back down. Especially effective when small or weak character has to use both hands to cock.

DAVID W. SMITH, *Westminister, Calif.*

COFKeyType (Computer Operation by Frenetic Keyboard Typing). In almost all movies involving the operation of computers, the user operates the machine by incongruent and frenetic banging on the keyboard, ignoring the mouse and system graphic interface elements. This results in instantaneous, nanosecond access and downloading of data. See *Jurassic Park, Disclosure.*

CARLOS GREENE, *Mexico City*

Coincidental Lighting. In any scene in a thriller involving a thunderstorm, when any character is looking for a pet or friend, there will be a deafening clap of thunder and a flash of lightning illuminating a corpse, or the murderer. If the character is searching for something, the lightning will illuminate the fact that the something is dramatically missing.

JIM LEE, *Cary, N.C.*

Cole Rule, The. No movie made since 1977 containing a character with the first name "Cole" has been any good. (Exception: *Days of Thunder,* which was good but not all that good.)

R. E.

Collapsing Display Trick. Pull one can from a pyramid, and they all fall onto the floor. Used by directors who set a scene in a store, and have nothing of substance to achieve there.

R. E.

Collapsing Staircase. When a character is rescued from a staircase during a disaster movie or thriller, the staircase always collapses the moment the rescue is completed.

SCOT MURPHY, *Highland Park, Ill.*

Coming and Going Attraction. If you've seen the trailer, you've seen the movie.

GREG BROWN, *Chicago*

Complimentary Dirt Rule. Explosions always enhance a star's looks by placing just the right touch of dirt across the cheekbones—never on the end of the nose.

BRENDA YOU, *Chicago*

Convenient Cat. Any time a good guy is being stealthy and knocks something over, alerting the bad guys, there will be a cat to take the rap. The guard will say, "Ahh, it was just the damned *cat!*" Note that this even works in scenes where a cat has no business being in the first place, such as a museum or computer room.

STEVE WIDEMAN

Cooperative Shooter Rule. No matter what kind of cover the hero hides behind, it will stop enemy bullets. In *Beverly Hills Cop 3*, Eddie Murphy uses a park bench for cover, and the bad guys shoot all the slats and none of the gaps.

DON HOWARD, *San Jose, Calif.*

Cooter Rule, The. When the young, good-looking hero goes back to his boyhood farmhouse, he'll inevitably have a fight at the dinner table with an older, less-attractive brother. The fight is usually about abandoning the farm and "spitting on Daddy's memory" or the hero's annoying use of correct grammar. The hero storms out of the house and sits down on a fence in the backyard. He is followed by his sweet, long-suffering sister-in-law. She says, "Trap, you're gonna have to forgive Cooter/Hunter/Trip/Billy Bob. He loves you. He don't mean nothin'. It's just his way, is all."

LISA STANSBURY, *Jacksonville, Fla.*

44

Corrupt Sheriff Rule. All sheriffs who are not the heroes of their movies are corrupt, and in the employ of the largest landowner in the area. Exception: If the sheriff is not corrupt he will be dead by the end of the movie.

JOE DiCOSTANZO, *New York City*

C. P. S. Rule. When a character drives somewhere in an overcrowded, gridlocked city such as L.A. or New York City, there is always a Convenient Parking Space directly in front of his destination.

JOHN JAKES, *Hilton Head Island, S.C.*

Crap Gap. The actor's mouth moves but the sound of his voice saying a dirty word has disappeared (thus, often making it sound as though he has the hiccups). Also known as "Beep Bleep" and "Inanity Profanity."

MERWYN GROTE, *St. Louis*

Creep Chord. The loud, discordant musical chord that is used in slasher movies to underline the moments, usually false alarms, when one character slips up behind another and scares him or her half to death. (Technical term: "Sting," or "stinger.")

R. E.

Creeper's Peepers. You can easily spot demonically possessed characters (or actual denizens of Hell) by their glowing red eyes. They seem to switch on involuntarily whenever the characters are alone, in shadow, thinking about how wonderfully evil they are.

MARK J. WOLMERING, *East Hartford, Conn.*

Creeping Doorknob. Any time there is a close-up shot of a doorknob, it will start turning very slowly, and usually without being noticed by a room's occupants—unless the occupants are trying to hide, in which case they will watch in horror as the knob turns.

RICK NEWBY, *College Place, Wash.*

Crime Sometimes Pays. Villains who outshine heroes are resurrected in sequels as quasi-good guys. Examples include King Kong, Godzilla, Jaws in the James Bond movies, the Terminator, and Rambo. Even more frightening: when villain become heroes by remaining villains (Freddie, Michael, and Jason).

MERWYN GROTE, *St. Louis*

Crystal Sideboard Rule. In any movie featuring an older businessman married to a younger woman, if his home or office contains a sideboard with cut-crystal decanters of dark spirits, there is a 50 percent chance the wife will be dead or in jeopardy by the end of the movie. These odds increase to 75 percent if the husband is played by William Devane, and to 100 percent if the movie is a "cable original."

DAWSON RAMBO, *Tucson, Ariz.*

Daddy's Girl Rule. Whenever a lead character is engaged to a rich girl who is his boss's daughter, by the end of the film he will have perpetrated a major screwup, lost his job, lost his fiancée, and gone off happily with somebody else.

IAN MANTGANI, *Liverpool, England*

Dawning Light Moment. The words "So *that's* what this is about!" in any movie invariably translate as, "you're cheating on me with someone else!"

R. E.

Deadly Change of Heart. When the cold heart of a villain softens and he turns into a good guy, the plot will quickly require him to be killed, usually after maudlin final words.

R. E.

Dead Man Dancing. Whenever the bad guy in a movie is holding a "dead man" switch that will set off a bomb if let go, the good guy will wrestle him for it, and together they will perform spectacular fights, stunts, and other gymnastics, falling down stairs and rolling out of the way of gunfire. During all this time, the switch is never released.

ROBERT EPPS, *Prather, Calif.*

Dead Man Talking. A character who is dead before the end of the movie is still allowed to narrate the film, making you believe he survives, as long as it moves the story forward. (E.g., Joe Pesci in *Casino,* William Holden in *Sunset Boulevard.*)

RHYS SOUTHAN, *Richardson, Tex.*

Dead Teenager Movie. Generic term for any movie primarily concerned with killing teenagers, without regard for logic, plot, performance, humor, etc. Often imitated, never worse than in the *Friday the 13th* sequels. Requires complete loss of common sense on the part of the characters. Sample dialogue: "All of our friends have been found horribly mutilated. It is midnight and we are miles from help. Hey, let's take off our clothes, walk through the dark woods, and go skinny-dipping!"

R. E.

Dead Werewolf Defense. In any horror film involving a human transforming into a monster, the hero never has to explain to the police the naked dead human body that is left after he has killed the monster. This despite the fact that no one in authority ever believes in the monster in the first place.

JOE DiCOSTANZO, *New York City*

Death is Wet. Every single morgue in a movie uses dripping or running water on the sound track.

R. E.

Del Close's Rule. Never share a foxhole with a character who carries a photo of his sweetheart.

DEL CLOSE, *Chicago*

Delta H of Crania. The factor in modern probability theory that accounts for the tendency of movie slot machines to pay off when smashed into headfirst by someone in a brawl. Can also be applied to actuarial systems involving jukeboxes that start playing appropriately ironic songs under similar conditions.

ANDY IHNATKO, *Westwood, Mass.*

Denim Safety. Ingenious handgun safety mechanism which automatically engages itself when the weapon is jammed into the waistband of a pair of jeans and automatically disengages itself when the weapon is drawn and the muzzle is clear of the actor's naughty bits.

ANDY IHNATKO, Westwood, Mass.

Deserting before Dessert. No one finishes a meal in the movies. Meals are interrupted by important calls, the appearance of an ex-lover, or a trivial argument. No one eats more than two bites of a hot dog, cotton candy, popcorn. If dessert is served, it will end up in someone's lap or dumped on his or her head. Only exception: STARVING MAN SCENE, which shows famished character polishing off the last speck of food, then placing his knife and fork on the plate to form an X.

MERWYN GROTE, St. Louis

Detour Rule. In any thriller, it is an absolute certainty that every road detour sign is a subterfuge to kidnap the occupants of a car. (Cf. Camel, Slow-Moving, "Hay Wagon!" etc.)

R. E.

Devolution in Action. Problem caused when highly competent parents, able to dodge burning meteors, falling buildings, etc., risk their lives to save idiot offspring, who respond to danger by moving toward it, whining "daddy!" when they see they've caught fire. These parents should focus on keeping themselves alive in order to breed fitter offspring.

MARY RILEY, Chicago

Dewey Decimal Dialogue. All conversations set in a library (1) involve at least one exchange between people standing on either side of a shelf and talking to each other through the stacks, and (2) always inspire at least one indignant "Shhhh!" from an elderly librarian. (2a) If a great many books must be carried anywhere in a character's arms, they will be dropped with a loud noise.

R. E.

Die Three Times Law. In modern movies it has become a law that the villain must die three times. First he gets killed–but isn't really dead! Then he gets killed–but he's still alive. Then he gets killed.

DAVID BURD, *East Stroudsburg, Pa.*

Difficult We Do Immediately, The. Usually happens in the middle of a movie, when the main characters build or repair something which would normally take weeks in about two minutes or less (example: refurbishing a boat which hasn't left the dock in twenty years). See *Six Days, Seven Nights*.

JIM SIMON, *Villa Park, Calif.*

Dirt Equals Virtue. In technology movies, a small, dingy, cluttered little lab and eccentric personnel equal high principles; large, well-lighted facilities mask sinister motives.

PAUL A. LEE, *Germantown, Ohio*

Disappearing Nude. A woman seen nude in bed with the hero in the opening scene will never be seen again.

DAVID STEVENS, *Irving, Tex.*

Disbelief of Suspension. Rope and plank bridges are never shown in a film unless they are going to fail. Ropes will be cut, burned, or frayed. In the case of planks, someone's foot will fall through the rotten wood.

LIBBY WEBSTER, Columbus, Ind.

Disclosing Whisper Law. If a character is looking for an object, and the audience doesn't know what the object is, the character will mumble it out loud to himself as he frantically searches for it. See *Mission Impossible*.

RHYS SOUTHAN, Richardson, Tex.

Disconnection. Any character who says, "I can't tell you over the phone . . ." doesn't have long to live, and will die at the rendezvous: (a) without uttering a word, (b) mumbling a red herring, or (c) giving an obtuse clue (e.g., "Beware of the dwarf" in *Foul Play*).

DON HOWARD, San Jose, Calif.

Disney Ethical Exception. The bad guys or "the team to beat" can cheat and win any time except in the Big Game. Then, no matter how tiny the infraction, he/she/they will be disqualified for not following the rules. However, underdogs can cheat and win at any time and never be questioned. This is the Disney Ethical Exception, so called after all the Disney films where the incompetent but lovable underdogs win because of bizarre inventions *(Son of Flubber)*, freak accidents *(The Computer Wore Tennis Shoes)*, supernatural powers *(The Love Bug)*, or magical potions *(The Strongest Man in the World)*.

MERWYN GROTE, St. Louis

Divine Dog Syndrome

Divine Dog Syndrome. In movies, humans are violently killed with impunity, but dogs are never killed. Thus, an alien race studying films would conclude that dogs are gods.

PAUL CASSEL

Docudrama. TV term for extended-length program which stars a disease or social problem and costars performers willing to give interviews on how they experienced personal growth through their dramatic contact with same.

R. E.

Dog Bites Man Rule. Whenever a character is asked to read an important story in a newspaper, he will inevitably provide a small laugh by reading the wrong story. In movies, no one is capable of scanning a headline and recognizing a story of personal consequence.

PAUL N. YERKEY, *Amherst, N.Y.*

Doggone It Rule. Movies put dogs in stories and then don't let them do what a real dog would do. See *Fatal Attraction,* where Michael Douglas's family owns a dog that is home during the noisy and gruesome bathtub scene but never comes sniffing around to investigate.

MARY STEINBERG, *Chicago*

Don't Just Save the Rain Forest—Recycle It! No matter what film you select from the classic Johnny Weismueller "Tarzan" series, one of these sequences will be present: (a) an elephant stampede or (b) Tarzan atop a

gigantic crocodile, over thirty feet long, and spinning end-
lessly over and over as he repeatedly stabs it. These are
literally the same sequences lifted in their entirety with
new reaction shots of the protagonists dropped in later for
continuity.

DAVID H. COLEMAN, *Tarzana, Calif.*

Don't Leave Home without It. A child's backpack invariably contains everything needed to survive most dis-
asters, and is also a help in traveling back in time. See *A
Kid in King Arthur's Court* and *Far from Home: Adventures
of Yellow Dog.*

PRILLIE HULS, *St. Joseph, Ill.*

**Don't Make Me Smile and Reveal How I Really Feel
Sequence.** This is an obligatory scene in any movie where
a man wants a woman to like him, and the woman thinks
she might like him but isn't sure, and the woman's child
already really likes the guy. Man and child are having fun
together when mom comes to the door and says to the
child, "Time for dinner." Pause, then fake-sternly, "Now!"

R. E.

Doomed Patient Dialogue. "Hey, wait a minute! You're
not my regular nurse!"

KIM ROTZOLL, *Urbana, Ill.*

Dorothy Lamour Syndrome. Token female character in
a scene with two male leads is reduced to looking back
and forth between the conversing males. Ms. Lamour had

Don't Just Save the Rain Forest—Recycle It!

an excuse—Hope and Crosby were usually off the script. Often seen in movies back to the 1940s; in *13 Rue Madeleine* the primary action taken by the lone female spy is to look back and forth in confusion while the two male spies argue just before a parachute jump.

LESA CAMPBELL

Dossier Rule. In a movie where the villain is a rogue CIA/KGB/special forces agent, invariably there is a scene where one of the good guys pulls out a folder stamped "Top Secret." The file contains a blurry photograph of the bad guy *(Apocalypse Now, Cliffhanger)*. Compare the "Slide Show Rule"—similar, except the head good guy has a magic lantern show, projects a blurry picture of the bad guy, and intones, "He's a former member of the KGB/IRA/Red Brigade" *(Nighthawks, In the Line of Fire)*.

CHRIS FISANICK, *Barnesboro, Pa.*

Double Step. In an extended dance scene or any other sequence in which a character must demonstrate professional skill, the absurdly simple opening move the actor learns for the close-up before they cut away to the highly trained double's virtuoso performance.

ANDY IHNATKO, *Westwood, Mass.*

Down Under Rule. No film set in Australia is allowed to use the word Australia in its title where "Down Under" is an acceptable alternative. For example, we don't get *The Rescuers in Australia* or *Quigley in Australia*.

STEPHEN ROWLEY, *Melbourne, Australia*

Dramatic Late Arrival Shot. A talented kid has a mother who forbids her to perform. The kid goes on anyway. Just when she's in the spotlight for her big number, the door opens at the back of the auditorium, and who walks in? The mother, of course, who in a later shot inevitably allows herself to relent, smile, and be proud of her kid after all.

R. E.

"Dr. Curie Will See You Now" Rule. Any time a character's gender is not identified until we have had time to make an assumption, it will turn out to be of the opposite gender. For example, a macho motorcycle rider negotiates a series of obstacles, rides up to the camera, and removes his helmet only to reveal–gasp!–that "he" is a "she!"

BRIAN JONES

Dressing Room Rule. In any scene where there is a dressing room in a store, the door or curtain will open to briefly reveal a secondary or supporting character, topless.

DAVID STEVENS, *Irving, Tex.*

Dr. Exposition, I Presume. All movie scientists who are neither the hero nor working for the bad guy are always doctors, and are, without fail, in the story only to present a crucial bit of information or explain some scientific concept to the hero, following which they are killed while doing further research on the problem.

BRANNON MOORE, *Seattle*

Duck Call Shortcut. All waterfowl in TV nature specials make the same sound, regardless of species. It is the sound

Dude's Landing

of a hunter's duck call, and is usually accompanied by the sound of fingers paddling around in water. No matter how much *National Geographic* spends to take pictures of our planet's thousands of duck species, they can't bear to spend more than ten bucks on a sound effect.

RAPHAEL CARTER, Tempe, Ariz.

Dude's Landing. In any movie where greenhorn city folks arrive in rugged terrain, there is always a scene of a grizzled local old-timer, his eyes narrowed, watching them arrive. He wisely foresees what they're in for.

R. E.

Ebert's Three Laws of Motion Pictures
1. A movie is not about what it is about, but about how it is about it.
2. No good movie is too long. No bad movie is short enough.
3. No good movie is depressing. All bad movies are depressing.

R. E.

8mm Omen. Films that start with old home movies are never about happy lives.

R. E.

Ellipses Principle. Any film that combines reviewers' quotes with ellipses can't be any good. A review that says "This movie was . . . amazing" probably read "This movie was so awful it is amazing how it ever got made." Reviews of

three words or less (e.g., "Funny . . . ," "What a movie . . .")
are especially cause for concern.

DAVE KALIN, *San Francisco*

Ellis's Law. A single African-American or Italian in a cast
of nonethnic people is usually a good guy. If a film contains more than four African-Americans or Italians in
speaking roles, they're all gang members. See *Lethal
Weapon* or *My Cousin Vinny* for positives, almost any
other film for negatives.

ANDY IHNATKO, *Westwood, Mass.*

Emergency Tour Guide. The person in every crowd at a
disaster scene who fully extends an arm to point at the
obvious thing that everyone is already looking at or running from. Example: The woman near the end of *Arma-
geddon* who points at the fireball in the sky that everyone
on the whole planet is already watching.

CHRIS JONES, *Snellville, Ga.*

Empathy Deficit Disorder. Affliction where film audiences can't seem to understand that not every scene in
which a character appears with a mental disorder is funny.
See Dustin Hoffman in *Rain Man* and Richard Gere in *Mr.
Jones.* The audiences I saw these movies with laughed
from start to finish, thinking if the character was mentally
ill and there was even one amusing scene, the entire
movie was slapstick comedy.

KATHLEEN WILSON, *Roanoke, Va.*

Empty Box Syndrome. Any car in a chase approaching
a wall of stacked boxes will not only invariably run into it,
but will find that the boxes are empty and scatter impres-
sively (which certainly wouldn't happen if boxes labeled,
say, "Air Conditioner" were actually full).

STEVEN RAIMI

End Credit Ratio. The longer the end credits are, the
more money there was spent on special effects, and the
less money there was spent on plot, characterization, and
dialogue.

DAWSON E. RAMBO, *Pelham Manor, N.Y.*

Ending, Giving Away the. Critics get hate mail from
readers when they reveal too much about the endings of
thrillers. Here is the ending of all thrillers: The bad guy
gets killed.

RICH ELIAS, *Delaware, Ohio*

Engine Equalization Law. Movie phenomenon which
allows large, lumbering Cadillac stretch limousines filled
with bad guys to keep up with heroes in exotic sports cars.

EDWARD SAVIO, *San Francisco*

Ennui Warned You. If a critic uses the word "ennui" positively in a review of any foreign film, the film will be a
pretentious bore, i.e., the collected works of Michelangelo
Antonioni.

MERWYN GROTE, *St. Louis*

Estrogen Trinity. The Holy Female Trinity in tear-jerking dramas, consisting of: (1) the heroine, who is shy and unsure of her own power as a human being; (2) the mentor, who is brash and outspoken and helps heroine acquire those same qualities; and (3) the corpse, the mother/daughter/sister/friend who announces during dinner that she's been diagnosed with a terminal illness and has less than three reels to live, who helps each of the others achieve perspective and maybe cop an Oscar for the funeral scene.

ANDY IHNATKO, *Westwood, Mass.*

Ethnic Defaults. All Asian people know karate. All Latin people dance salsa. Any Russian character is related to some ex-KGB agent now working for the new Russian Mafia.

ALEXIS S. MENDEZ, *Aguadilla, Puerto Rico*

E.T. Ratio. The more coverage *Entertainment Tonight* gives to a big stunt (such as the explosions in *Lethal Weapon, Blown Away,* and *The Specialist,* the fall in *Terminal Velocity,* or any chase scene), the greater the likelihood the stunt will be the only thing in the film worth seeing.

MERWYN GROTE, *St. Louis*

Eventually Suspicious Unsuspecting Suspect. He doesn't know anything, but they think he does. He'll probably never know anything, but they abduct and interrogate him at gunpoint, so they can find out what he knows. He somehow escapes, and motivated by his terrifying experience, he eventually finds out not only what they thought he knew, but everything else.

RYAN WHITNEY, *Washington, D.C.*

Everybody's a Critic. Any painting, sculpture, tapestry, or other piece of artwork that receives more than one compliment from a supporting character (the more ridiculously effusive the better), or gets more than five seconds of uninterrupted screen time, or both, will be burned, slashed, shattered, defaced, or otherwise destroyed by the end of the film.

BRANNON MOORE, *Seattle*

"Everyone's Talking" Rule. If a movie ad portrays happy theater patrons exiting the movie and extolling the film's virtues, the movie itself will invariably be terrible.

DOUGLAS M. GARROU, *Seattle*

Evil Corporation Rule. Whenever a crusading movie character of extreme moral virtue uncovers a plot by an evil corporation to endanger public health for the sake of greed, the security department of this corporation will always have its own team of staff assassins who will use a black sedan to chase the hero in an assassination attempt.

TIM BENTON, *Huntsville, Ala.*

Explosion ESP. The characters always know whether the crashed and smoldering vehicle they are in will explode. If they don't get out and run, it won't explode. If they do, it does.

KYLE L. CAIN, *Sugar Land, Tex.*

Explosion Loop. Every explosion is shown at least three times, from three different angles, and the sound track has three "booms" on it, even though it's only one explosion.

DON HOWARD, *San Jose, Calif.*

EZ Open Gift Rule. Any time a gift-wrapped present is unwrapped in a movie, it's always easily opened by lifting a separately wrapped lid.

KYLE L. CAIN, *Sugar Land, Tex.*

Factory Confrontation (similar to the Far-Off Rattle Movie). The final battle between the hero and the villain must take place in a factory or stockyard, preferably one with lots of heavy machinery or fire or molten materials. Examples include the *RoboCop, Lethal Weapon,* and *Terminator* pictures.

DAVE KALIN, *San Francisco*

Fallacy of Elaborate Death Techniques. Any method of attempting to kill someone in a movie that is more complicated than shooting, beating, strangling, etc., will inevitably fail. (Cf. James Bond's many escapes.)

STEVE HORNE

Fallacy of the Beeping Radar. In every movie wherein a radar scope is shown, when the sweep passes over the target of interest, the radar beeps. Radar screens don't beep. Not now, not ever.

GRANT SIGSWORTH, *San Diego, Calif.*

Fallacy of the Predictable Tree. The logical error committed every time the good guy is able to predict exactly what the bad guy is going to do. For example, in *First Blood,* law enforcement officials are searching the woods for John Rambo. A cop pauses under a tree. Rambo drops on him. Question: Out of all the trees in the forest, how did Rambo know which one the guy would pause under?

R. E.

Fallacy of the Talking Killer. The villain wants to kill the hero. He has him cornered at gunpoint. All he has to do is pull the trigger. But he always talks first. He explains the hero's mistakes to him. Jeers. Laughs. And gives the hero time to think his way out of the situation, or be rescued by his buddy. (Cf. most James Bond movies.)

GENE SISKEL

Falling Chess Board Phenomenon. In any movie about a chess fanatic, the chess board that is perpetually set up in his office will always get knocked over by the end of the movie.

DOUG FLETCHER, *Mesa, Ariz.*

Falling Death Scream Rule. Any character falling to his or her death must scream on the way down, especially if he or she is a villain. If no scream is heard, chances are the character survives the fall.

GERALD FITZGERALD, *Dallas*

Fallacy of the Predictable Tree

Falling Villain, The. At the end of virtually every action-adventure movie, the villain must fall from a great height onto a hard surface. If possible, the villain should crash backward through a plate-glass window and land on an automobile.

STEPHEN D. DARGITZ, Ann Arbor, Mich.

False Relaxation Reflex. If the film's top villain places his hand on a henchman's shoulder (very important) and tells him not to worry about having screwed up, the henchman will be dead in less than a minute of screen time.

JASON MOORE

Far-Off Rattle Movies. Movies in which the climactic scene is shot in a deserted warehouse, where far-off rattles punctuate the silence.

R. E.

Fast Food Rule. Wanna know what the summer's block-buster is going to be? See who McDonald's does the marketing tie-in with. Wanna know what blockbuster will do disappointing business? See who Burger King ties in with.

DAWSON E. RAMBO, Pelham Manor, N.Y.

Fatal Basic Attraction Instinct Genre. Movies about sex between bad people who live in good houses.

R. E.

Fat Man Formula. In all movies where groups of men live together, it is always the fat one who cannot be trusted. See *No Escape*.

R. E.

Feedback Rule. Every time anyone uses a microphone in a movie, it feeds back.

ARDEN J. COOPER, *Warren, Mich.*

Feline Fright. When a movie hero/heroine is wandering down any dark and deserted alley, he/she will inevitably be frightened by a cat before encountering the villain.

DAVE KALIN, *San Francisco*

Female Shoot and Cry Rule. Except in movies where the lead is a tough female, any female character who shoots the bad guy for any reason will then drop the gun, bend at the knees, and start sobbing.

GREG BARNARD

Female Star in a Topless Bar Rule. If a movie has a scene in a topless bar, the film's female star will never be seen nude in the movie, unless she is a topless dancer.

DAVID STEVENS, *Irving, Tex.*

Female Voice of Destruction. If the auto-destruction feature is activated at a secret base or spaceship, the countdown is always announced by a female voice. See *Aliens, Sphere,* James Bond movies, etc.

ALEXIS S. MENDEZ, *Aguadilla, Puerto Rico*

Fifty-five-gallon Drum Rule. Fifty-five-gallon drums are a culturally rooted symbol of evil, because they usually contain a substance with a long name that we can't identify. The more drums, the more evil.

PAUL A. LEE, *Germantown, Wis.*

Fireball Law of Physics. "The speed of an expanding fireball is in direct relation to the running speed of the slowest major star moving away from the fireball. If FS = Fireball Speed, and RS = Running Star, therefore (FS = [RS × 9]). Since fireballs have actually been slowing down recently to accommodate slower stars, even *Grumpiest Old Men* may be able to work in a fireball.

ED DOBEAS and KRISTEN KIRKHAM, *Seattle*

First Law of Alien Contact. They send signals to our huge radio antennae only on cloudless nights. See *Contact, Species.*

PATRICK SUAREZ, *Springfield, Ohio*

First Law of Funny Names. No names are funny unless used by W. C. Fields or Groucho Marx. Funny names, in general, are a sign of desperation at the screenplay level. (E.g., "Dr. Hfuhruhurr" in *The Man With Two Brains.*)

R. E.

First Rule of Repetition of Names. When the same names are repeated in a movie more than four times a minute for more than three minutes in a row, the audience breaks out into sarcastic laughter, and some of the ruder members are likely to start shouting "Kirsty!" and "Tiffany!" at the screen. See *Hellbound: Hellraiser II*.

R. E.

First Rule of Whodunits. In any murder mystery, the murderer is probably the person who offers the most assistance in finding the killer.

GERALD FITZGERALD, Dallas

First Time's the Charm. Ninety-nine percent of sex scenes show couples coupling for the first time.

NIGEL SEARLE, Venice, Fla.

Five Minute Class, The. No scene showing a class in session ever lasts more than five minutes. Even the most stimulating session is invariably interrupted by the bell.

DENNIS WARD

Flint Content in Metal. During sword fights, showers of sparks are produced whenever the weapons clang into each other.

MARK J. WOLMERING, East Hartford, Conn.

Floating Luggage. In every scene where actors carry luggage, the luggage is obviously empty. They attempt, with pained expressions on their faces, to pretend the bags are heavy, and yet they can flick them around like feathers.

TOM KIRKPATRICK, Chicago

Flying Felines of Fear. Inevitably appearing in every Dead Teenager Movie since the dawn of time, some hapless victim is scared witless by the sudden appearance of a cat which has apparently been flung at the actor by some off-camera stagehand.

BRET HAYDEN, Los Angeles

"Food Fight!" Dialogue which replaced "Westward ho!" as American movies ended the long frontier trek and began to look inward for sources of inspiration.

R. E.

Footlocker Scene. In many action movies, there's a scene toward the end where the hero digs into a dusty footlocker. Inside are: (a) yellowing photographs of the hero and his buddies in the last "unpopular" war; (b) old camouflage uniforms; (c) medals awarded for valor, still in their presentation boxes; and (d) an exotic weapon that is illegal in most states, which the hero grimly begins to assemble.

DAWSON RAMBO, Tucson, Ariz.

Four Glass Movie. Any movie with a plot that can be summarized on four souvenir soft drink containers from McDonald's. See also "Fast Food Rule."

R. E.

Four-Letter Rating Upgrade. Practice of inserting totally gratuitous obscenities into otherwise clean-cut family films in order to avoid the dreaded "G" rating. Classic example: "Penis breath" in *E.T.*

MERWYN GROTE, *St. Louis*

Fourth Out, The. Anyone displaying an extremely rare baseball card will, within three minutes, see it lost, stolen, torn up, burned, or otherwise destroyed. Similarly, any valuable objet d'art made of flammable or breakable material is likewise doomed. (A resourceful filmmaker can drag this out into an entire feature, e.g., *Bean*).

MICHAEL SCHLESINGER, *Culver City, Calif.*

Four-to-Three Keyboard Rule. When the camera is focused on a computer screen, it takes four keyboard clicks to produce every three characters.

JIM COLLIER, *Dallas*

Fractured Festivities. The character called upon to save the nation from a terrorist threat will be summoned from his grade-schooler's birthday party. And at least one other government official will be attending a formal social function when he's called to the situation room, ensuring that he'll be wearing evening clothes for the rest of the movie.

TRISHA JOHNSTON, *Walnut Creek, Calif.*

Friendly Fire Tabu. Inevitably, in an action film, a situation will arise where the protagonist almost shoots his partner or is nearly shot by him. Of course, the trigger is never pulled, and the target is recognized as "friendly" just milliseconds before firing, even though visibility is poor, the partner appears on the scene totally unexpected and possibly in disguise, and is pointing a loaded gun! Typically, the two parties have some personal beef with one another that won't be resolved until a later scene.

ROBERT BEMBEN, *Ann Arbor, Mich.*

Friendly Neighborhood Skies Syndrome. In "test pilot" films, the fatal crash of the experimental aircraft that occurs in the last reel is always on the aircraft's home field—and no more than 500 yards from the observation point where the pilot's girlfriend is watching.

RICHARD KUNZ, *Chicago*

Front Row Formula. The character playing the leading role in a movie always stands in front of a group of people, for example in an aerobics lesson.

BOB LEFEVERE

Frozen Family Phenomenon. Applies to movies such as *Homeward Bound,* in which the family has lost a minimum of three pets. Family stands looking toward the hill as they think they hear barking. One pet comes over the hill. No one moves. Instead of running toward the hilltop to see if the next pet will appear, the family remains motionless as the second pet arrives. Then family remains frozen until, after suspenseful delay, finally the third pet appears. Arrival of third pet gives permission for family to leap into motion.

LINDA TILLMAN, *Atlanta*

"Fruit Cart!" An expletive used by knowledgeable film buffs during any chase scene involving a foreign or ethnic locale, reflecting their certainty that a fruit cart will be overturned during the chase, and an angry peddler will run into the middle of the street to shake his fist at the hero's departing vehicle.

R. E.

"Fruit Cart!" (James Bond Variation). In Bond movies, chase scenes not only upset applecarts, but Agent 007 also invariably plows whatever vehicle he is piloting through the buffet table at an outdoor wedding reception. This is a commentary of Bond's attitude toward monogamy (at least until *Licence to Kill,* when a chase scene ends with Bond parachuting into a DEA agent's wedding to serve as best man.)

ANTHONY BRUCE GILPIN, *Riverside, Calif.*

Fudd Flag. In the background field of an animated cartoon, the one slightly differently painted object (floorboard, cupboard door, rock) among a dozen otherwise identical background objects. This is so Bugs Bunny will know which floorboard his rabbit hole is under, Tom will know which cupboard he'll have to open in order to be bludgeoned by Jerry with a frying pan, and Wile E. Coyote can unerringly choose to cling to the most break-offable piece of rock on the cliff face.

ANDY IHNATKO, *Westwood, Mass.*

Futile Hug Syndrome. If it's "next morning" and there's a close shot of a person in bed asleep, he or she will wake up, and turn with arm outstretched as if to hug the person lying there, but will always find an empty space, as his or her partner has been up hours fixing breakfast/taking the dog out/exercising/being murdered.

MICHELLE MENDOZA, *Chalfont St. Giles, Bucks, England*

Gandhi Movie. Any film which is undeniably good, perhaps great, but once you've seen it, there is absolutely no reason to ever want to see it again. Examples: *Gandhi, The Last Emperor, A Passage to India,* long documentaries about the Holocaust, most of the French New Wave, all underground art films of the 1960s, the lesser works of Bergman and Antonioni, and Woody Allen's "serious" movies.

MERWYN GROTE, *St. Louis*

Geek Ego Effect. Exemplified by the Dennis Nedry character in *Jurassic Park,* this describes the maniacal behavior of the mandatory nerd with thick glasses, pocket protector, and an I'll-get-even-with-the-rest-of-the-world-for-not-taking-me-seriously attitude.

FRED DECKER

Gender Offender Temporal Paradox. In films set in the present, male characters act like they're from several eras in the past and get punched out by women afterward as a direct result. In films set several eras in the past, female characters act like they're from the present but never get punched out afterward as a direct result.

ANDY IHNATKO, *Westwood, Mass.*

75

Gentleman Villain

Generation Squeeze. Hollywood genre which tries to bridge the generation gap by creating movies which will appeal to teenagers at the box office and to adults at the video rental counter. Typical plot device: An adult becomes a teenager, or vice versa (cf. *Like Father, Like Son; Hiding Out; Peggy Sue Got Married; Vice Versa; 18 Again; Big*). Also sometimes masquerades as a movie apparently about adults, but with young actors in the "adult" roles (cf. *No Man's Land, The Big Town*).

R. E.

Generic Drinker Syndrome. Characters in movies always order "beer." As a bartender, I have observed that people never just order "beer." They always call their beer. Movie characters frequently take a small sip and then leave without finishing their drinks or paying for them (occasionally one character will throw some uncounted bills on the table). In real life, people suddenly called away from the bar take time to upend their glass and greedily suck down whatever is left.

Lauri Jackson-Sickler, *Edmonds, Wash.*

Gentleman Villain. Any head of a large organization who speaks with perfect, condescending diction and wears elegant, custom-fitted suits is the villain.

G. W. Roles, *Washington, D.C.*

Ghost-Repellent Realtors. Even though ghosts desperately want to keep anyone from occupying the houses they haunt, they never bother to show up until the new owners have signed on the dotted line. Since rattling chains during the Open House would save them a lot of trouble, it is obvious that ghosts are repelled by real-estate agents.

RAPHAEL CARTER, *Tempe, Ariz.*

Gibson's Inverse Coefficient of Gravity. Force of nature which affects firearms of good guys as they scale tall buildings. Force grows geometrically greater the higher up the good guy is, eventually causing firearm to fall irretrievably from his grasp when he needs it most. (Fun Fact: This force generates a powerful visual aura, causing good guy to waste precious time watching firearm fall all the way to the ground while he's in immediate peril.)

ANDY IHNATKO, *Westwood, Mass.*

Give Me Some Feedback. Whenever an inexperienced or reluctant public speaker steps up to the microphone, he is greeted with a shrill blast of feedback when he begins to speak.

BOBBY SKAFISH, *Chicago*

Glowing Dashboard Phenomenon. Everyone in the movies who drives a car at night has a bright light somewhere on the dashboard that's aimed at his or her face. No wonder people drive so wildly in films: They can't see!

GORDON HAMMERLE, *Adrian College, Adrian, Mich.*

Go Ahead and Jump. That big fall will never kill the hero. See *Butch Cassidy and the Sundance Kid, Lethal Weapon, Last of the Mohicans, The Fugitive, Ravenous.*

CHRISTOPHER M. TERRY, *Atlanta, Ga.*

Godot Movie. Movie in which the producers think that if they just put some big-name comic actors in an oddball situation, something funny is bound to happen eventually (e.g., Robin Williams, Whoopi Goldberg, and Bette Midler as space pirates!). The audience sits through the whole production waiting for laughs that never come.

ANDY IHNATKO, Westwood, Mass.

Good Bad Guy. Crook you are allowed to root for only because this is his last job, after which he will either retire or establish the restaurant of his dreams.

ALEXIS S. MENDEZ, Aguadilla, Puerto Rico

Gotham Sentence. When a character learns the hero's secret identity, one of two standard movie punishments will result: (a) death or (b) sex with the hero.

ANDY IHNATKO, Westwood, Mass.

Grace Under Fire Principle. Any female character who claims to abhor violence will, during the film's conclusion, shoot the bad guy who has the drop on her boyfriend/husband. After firing, she must hold the gun up in her trembling hand for two seconds or until her man takes it from her without so much as a "thank you." Named for Grace Kelly in *High Noon*.

CHRISTOPHER M. TERRY, Atlanta, Ga.

Gradually Gathering Guffaw. The setup: A bad guy, surrounded by henchmen, is confronted by the hero, who insolently insults him. There is a pregnant pause, during which instant violence seems likely. Cut to: the villain, who pauses for two beats, and then laughs. Cut to: his top henchman, who glances at the boss, waits two more beats, and then laughs too. Cut to: all the other bad guys, joining in the laughter. (Alternate close: The villain cuts his laugh short and inflicts unexpected pain upon either the good guy or one of his own henchmen.)

R. E.

Grafik Artz. Banner, sign, or any other handmade drawing which purportedly has been made by untrained hands but which obviously was the expensive work of professional artists. Use of Grafik Artz is usually betrayed by the perfect lines, circles, and randomly reversed letters in a child's drawing, or a picket sign at an "impromptu" grassroots rally which is silkscreened in two-color Dom Casual.

ANDY IHNATKO, *Westwood, Mass.*

Grave Talk. Handy screenwriter's tool where a character can reveal his personality and motivation by explaining everything to a tombstone.

PHIL HEINK, *Lexington, Ky.*

Great Eggs-Pectations. In old movies, after suffering through an ordeal, the heroine invariably suggests breakfast. The subject of eggs will naturally arise. If the heroine offers the hero cold eggs (i.e., an egg salad sandwich), there will be no sex now, but maybe later. If she offers to just "cook" or "fix" a couple of eggs, romance is likely. Fried eggs (sizzling and sunny-side up) means casual sex. Scrambled eggs means "watch out!" If omelets are mentioned, marriage or a long-term relationship is in the offing. If he offers to prepare the eggs, a commitment has been made.

MERWYN GROTE, *St. Louis*

Grenades Choose Sides. When a hand grenade falls near a good guy, he is able to: (a) pick it up before it detonates and throw it back to the issuing bad guy, or (b) run and leap out of the path of exploding shrapnel, usually in slow motion. But when a bad guy is on the receiving end of a grenade, all he can muster is a shocked expression before being blown to bits.

NEIL MARTIN, *Dartmouth, Mass.*

Grim Reaping. Involuntary and unconscious act of counting up the cast members in old movies who are no longer alive. For instance, seeing *Gone With the Wind* and reflecting that everybody in it is dead except for Butterfly McQueen. Particularly distracting if you think Butterfly McQueen might have died too.

MERWYN GROTE, *St. Louis*

Group Therapy Movie. Characters are trapped in close quarters to squeeze several years of intensive psychotherapy into a few hours of arguing, partying, or violence. See *The Big Chill, The Breakfast Club, The Men's Club, The Women, Steaming, Streamers, The Boys in the Band, Who's Afraid of Virginia Woolf?, Glengarry Glen Ross, Long Day's Journey into Night,* etc.

MERWYN GROTE, *St. Louis*

Gullible Entendre. Scene where the audience is expected to believe that two characters can carry on an entire conversation where one thinks they're discussing something like mathematics or banking, but the other thinks they're discussing sex. See *Milk Money, Frozen Assets,* reruns of *Three's Company.*

CHRISTOPHER P. NICHOLSON, *Sterling, Va.*

GUNDAN Movie. Any movie that Goes Nowhere and Does Nothing. Named in honor of the many pipes and conduits in starships on *Star Trek,* which have official-looking technical labels reading "GNDN." This is an in-joke; when the set designer was asked where those conduits were supposed to lead and what their functions were, he responded that they Go Nowhere and Do Nothing.

ANDY IHNATKO, *Westwood, Mass.*

Gun Disposal Rule. The character pulls the trigger, but the gun only clicks, because it's empty. So, the character throws it away. Obviously, it will never be needed again.
Explained by JIM JARMUSCH *in* Blue in the Face.

Haircut Hierarchy Rule. The main character in a movie centering around the military or prison never has the same severe crew cut that the other characters have, even though there is usually the obligatory haircut scene (e.g., Matthew Broderick in *Biloxi Blues,* Tom Cruise in *Top Gun,* Robert Redford in *Brubaker*). See also "Barber's Itch Rule."

JIM RACHEFF

Half Nude Rule. People in movies *always* undress from the top down. Especially women.

BILL BECWAR, *Wauwatosa, Wis.*

Hand-in-Hand Rule. In many Hollywood action pictures, the woman characters are incapable of fleeing from danger unless dragged by a strong man, who takes the woman's hand and pulls her along meekly behind him. This convention is so strong it appears even in films where it makes no sense, such as *Sheena,* in which a jungle-woman who has ruled the savage beasts since infancy is pulled along by a TV anchorman fresh off the plane.

R. E.

Hangman's Eye View. When someone is going to be hung, the shot will start with a view of the crowd, then zoom back to show that the audience is looking through the noose hanging on the scaffold. See *Robin Hood, Prince of Thieves.*

MICHAEL P. FAETH

Hans Zimmer Rides Again. An astonishingly high percentage of music in movie trailers feature Hans Zimmer's scores from *Backdraft* or *Crimson Tide.*

WILL GRIFFIN, *Bristol, England*

Hardest Word in the English Language. No matter how well a foreigner speaks English, he will never be able to master "yes," and will invariably be forced to rely on its equivalent in his native tongue.

EMO PHILLIPS, *Chicago*

Hand-in-Hand Rule

Harrison Door. Special automated door or barrier, ostensibly designed for high security but which nonetheless moves into place slowly and methodically instead of swiftly and efficiently, thus allowing the escape of celebrities. Harrison Doors are equipped with special sensors triggered by personal charisma, which explains how the hero of a picture set on a crippled undersea vessel manages to squeak past the automatically closing emergency watertight hatch while his comrades drown just behind him. (Named for Harrison Ford, who, whether in danger of being trapped by a thousand-year-old stone door fifty years ago in South America or by a set of bulletproof doors today in Chicago, has always been its single biggest beneficiary.)

ANDY IHNATKO, *Westwood, Mass.*

Harrison Ford Situational Reassessment Doubletake. Scene where Harrison Ford chases a small number of bad guys. He then stops suddenly, his expression changes to one of shock, and he runs back the way he came, as we see that the bad guys have been joined by a large number of reinforcements. See *Star Wars, Indiana Jones and the Temple of Doom.*

JEFF CROSS, *Marblehead, Mass.*

"Hay Wagon!" Rural Version of "Fruit Cart!" (q.v.). At the beginning of chase scenes through colorful ethnic locales, knowledgeable film buffs anticipate the inevitable scene in which the speeding sports car will get stuck on a narrow country lane behind a wagon overloaded with hay.

R. E.

Head Butt Rule. Whenever a head butt is delivered in a movie, the receiver of the butt is sent reeling into a semi-conscious stagger with all manner of hideous facial contusions, while the deliverer of the butt doesn't even wince, even though his own head has just received an identical impact.

TIM BENTON, *Huntsville, Ala.*

Heads Up Rule. Whenever a long-lost or secret grave site is discovered and exposed (the final scoops done by hand), the skull is always the first thing uncovered. See *Twilight.*

ROBERT HAYNES-PETERSON, *New York, N.Y.*

Helmet Hair. No woman in the movies ever puts up her hair before donning a motorcycle helmet, and yet when she removes the helmet, her inevitably long hair is not sweaty or tangled, but always perfectly styled.

ALESSANDRA KELLEY, *Chicago*

Hero Cop Identification Rule. In low-budget direct-to-video and cable movies, if you don't recognize any of the names of the actors in the opening credits, here's how to find the hero of the movie in the first few scenes. If there's an establishing shot of the bullpen or squad room, the hero is the one dressed in jeans, cowboy boots, and a leather bomber jacket, while all the other cops are in suits and ties. An even quicker way to identify the hero: He hasn't shaved in three days.

DAWSON RAMBO, *Pelham Manor, N.Y.*

Hey! Cody! Rule. Bad guy has drop on good guy. Can pull trigger and kill him. Inevitably shouts, "Hey! Cody!" (fill in name of good guy), after which good guy whirls, sees him, and shoots him first.

R. E.

Hollywood Car. Looks like a normal automobile, but backfires after being purchased from used car lot by movie heroine who is starting out again in life and is on her own this time.

R. E.

Hollywood Cigarette. In action thrillers where the hero smokes, he only lights one up to snap it angrily away after one or two puffs. Examples: Bruce Willis in *The Last Boy Scout* and Nick Nolte in *48 HRS* and *Another 48 HRS,* among countless others.

DAWSON E. RAMBO, *Pelham Manor, N.Y.*

Hollywood Cop Car. Driven by the slovenly member of the team in all police versions of the Opposites in Collision plot. Always unspeakably filthy, dented, rusty, and containing all of the cop's possessions in the back seat, as well as several weeks' worth of fast-food wrappers. Usually, but not necessarily, some kind of distinctive make or model (Gremlin, old Ford woody wagon, beat-up Caddy convertible, 4 × 4 van, etc.).

R. E.

Hollywood Flavor of the Month. Compulsion by studios to cast the hottest actor of the moment in a coveted role, regardless of whether the actor conforms to the look or style the original author had in mind for the character. (Example: In Avery Corman's novel *Oh God!* the hero is a paunchy, balding, middle-aged Jewish freelance reporter from New York City. In the movie, this character is turned into a WASP supermarket employee from Long Beach, Calif., played by John Denver.)

ANTHONY BRUCE GILPIN, *Riverside, Calif.*

Hollywood Grocery Bags. Whenever a scared, cynical woman who never wants to fall in love again is pursued by an ardent suitor who wants to breach her wall of loneliness, she will go grocery shopping. Her bags will always break to (1) symbolize the mess her life is in, or (2) so that the suitor can help her pick up the pieces of her life and her oranges.

CINDY L. CUP CHOY, *Honolulu, Hawaii*

Hollywood Hospital. Where people go to die. Victim checks in, doesn't check out, because screen time is too valuable for characters to go into the hospital only to recover a few scenes later. Dialogue clue: When any seemingly able-bodied character uses the word "doctor," especially in a telephone conversation not intended to be overheard, he or she will be dead before the end of the film.

GENE SISKEL

Hollywood Strip Club. Strip clubs in the movies always feature women who have recently appeared in *Playboy.* They also always feature cages, and the dancers perform elaborate dances complete with costumes, props, and associated thematic music. In reality, most strippers are not ex-*Playboy* models, wear cheap lingerie, and dance listlessly to the same twenty heavy-metal songs while sneering at the patrons for loose dollars.

DAWSON RAMBO, Pelham Manor, N.Y.

Hollywood Television. When a TV is part of the set dressing, but is not integral to the plot, the chances are good that it will be playing a Western in black and white, just before or during the cavalry charge, complete with Indian war cries and bugles. The chances of this being true approach 100 percent if (a) the character watching the TV is a cop, and (b) he or she is waking up at three in the morning, following a drunken binge after losing his or her partner, badge, wife/husband, or all of the above.

DAWSON E. RAMBO, Pelham Manor, N.Y.

Honor Code Rule. In any movie set in either a military academy or a prep school, if the school's "Honor Code" is mentioned within five minutes of the opening credits, it is required that the hero will have to violate the code, motivated by a higher morality, and then: (a) The school officials will begin proceedings to expel the hero; (b) his friends will all look guiltily the other way; (c) the school will come to see the hero's point of view; or (d) his friends will come to his support. See *The Lords of Discipline, School Ties, Taps, Scent of a Woman,* etc.

DAWSON E. RAMBO, Pelham Manor, N.Y.

Horny Teenager Movie. Any film primarily concerned with teenage sexual hungers, usually male. Replaced, to a degree, by Dead Teenager Movies (q.v.), but always popular with middle-aged movie executives, who like to explain to their seventeen-year-old starlets why the logic of the dramatic situation and the teachings of Strasberg require them to remove their brassieres. (Cf. *Blame It on Rio, She's Out of Control.*)

R. E.

Hot Dog Rule. Whenever one or more police officers stop for a bite to eat, usually at a hot dog stand or greasy spoon diner, a crime is about to be committed. The officer never gets to take more than one bite of his sandwich before dropping it to pursue the suspect.

JOHN ANGELO, *New York, N.Y.*

Hot Justice Syndrome. All trials that are held south of the Mason-Dixon Line take place during the summer in a non–air-conditioned courtroom filled with people airing themselves with fans from a funeral home. Heroic lawyer always mops neck with big white handkerchief. Slimy defense attorney never sweats.

ANDY BUCK, *Farmington, Conn.*

Hot Tub Rules. If a hot tub is seen in a movie, people will take their clothes off and get in it. If the women have large breasts, it's a T&A movie. If the women have small breasts, it's a drama or a foreign film. If the women keep their underwear on, it's a coming-of-age movie. If it's a slasher movie or a thriller, there will be an electrical appliance located nearby.

DAVID STEVENS, *Irving, Tex.*

Huh? What? Ending. A film climax that should wrap up everything, but only perplexes because of a plot development that is clumsy, lame, illogical, or pretentious. Example: *Unforgiven,* which ends a two-hour sermon against vigilante violence with a twenty-minute celebration of vigilante violence. Other examples: The "who is the real killer" endings of *Cruising, Jagged Edge,* and *Basic Instinct.*

MERWYN GROTE, *St. Louis*

Human Antennae. Movie characters who have an amazing ability to turn on the TV precisely at the moment when a newscaster begins a report on something directly relating to them.

JEFFREY GRAEBNER

Hungry Harry Rule. A cop shows he is tough, unaffected, or just plain ambivalent by grabbing a quick bite to eat and munching while examining the scene of a grisly murder.

SCOT MURPHY, *Highland Park, Ill.*

Hunter's Walk. Whenever the hero enters an unknown dangerous place, he spends so much time looking behind him, lest he get jumped from the rear, that he ends up walking backward, and backs into the thing he's looking for. See Kirk's search of Regula One in *Star Trek II* or any Dead Teenager Movie.

JAMES M. CURRAN, *Bloomfield, N.J.*

Hypo Display Principle. Any character planning to administer a hypodermic needle must first shoot some of the antidote/poison/drug up into the air before sticking patient with it, no matter how carefully measured the dosage is.

KRISTINA GAJE, *Toms River, N.J.*

Idiot Plot. Any plot containing problems which would be solved instantly if all of the characters were not idiots.

Originally defined by JAMES BLISH

If Anything Happens to Them, We Can Hold a Benefit. In any film where a monster, villain, or natural disaster threatens the lives of the rich guests as a charity benefit, the mayor or other official will insist the benefit must not be canceled. See *Mighty Joe Young, The Relic,* many Batman movies, etc.

R. E.

Ihnatko's First Law of Egress. When you begin to notice and anticipate the little circles in the upper right corner of the frame signaling time for a reel change, it's time to see if you can sneak into another theater at the multiplex.

ANDY IHNATKO, *Westwood, Mass.*

Ihnatko's Law of Voice Recognition. A movie computer sufficiently advanced to allow real-time voice communication between itself and a human will nevertheless speak like a drunk who has just received a serious blow to the head.

ANDY IHNATKO, *Westwood, Mass.*

Illuminated Hello Rule. Whenever a character in a movie gets a telephone call in the middle of the night, he or she inevitably always turns on the light next to the bed before answering the phone. In real life, most people pick up the phone in the dark, but in the movies that would mean the camera couldn't photograph them.

GEORGE M. IACONO, *Chicago*

Impalement Principle. Whenever a sharp object is even remotely hinted at on the screen, someone will be impaled on it. See *Ricochet, Red Rock West,* and *Dead Again.*

DAVE KALIN, *San Francisco*

Impatient Groom Syndrome. Undesirable movie weddings are always hurried along by an impatient groom, especially if the groom is the villain and the bride is the protagonist's true love.

RHYS SOUTHAN, *Richardson, Tex.*

Imperial Storm Trooper Marksmanship Academy. Institution where movie thugs get their weapons training. Teaches them how to stand five abreast, firing automatic weapons into a small room, without hitting anyone inside. Also applies to bad-guy fighter pilots, bad-guy archers, even bad-guy martial artists. Role models are the menacing but incompetent plastic-suited thugs from the *Star Wars* films. Originally defined in role-playing game named "GURPS," by Steve Jackson Games.

LON MILLER, *Bloomington, Minn.*

Impregnable Fortress Impregnated. Indispensable scene in all James Bond movies and many other action pictures, especially war films. The IFI sequence begins early in the picture, with long shots of a faraway fortress and Wagnerian music on the sound track. Eventually the hero gains entry to the fortress, which is inevitably manned by technological clones in designer uniforms. Sequence ends with destruction of fortress, as clones futilely attempt to save their marvelous machines. See *The Guns of Navarone,* etc.

R. E.

Inanity Profanity. Nonsense words are dubbed over profanity (i.e., "god-damned son-of-a-bitch" turns into "green-toed son of a fish"). In *Last Action Hero,* virtually all of Frank MacRae's dialogue is cleverly scripted Inanity Profanity; and films like *Semi-Tough* are actually much funnier on television because of profanity that is totally inane. But hearing Peter Finch say "bullsoup" in the TV version of *Network* is inexcusable. See also "Beep Bleep" and "Crap Gap."

MERWYN GROTE, *St. Louis*

Indecisive Disappointment Rule. Screenwriter filled with feelings but short on words has character say, "Yes, No. I don't know." Alternate: "I don't know what to think any more."

WILL GRIFFIN, *Bristol, England*

Indoor Free Fall Phenomenon. When a character falls through the floor in a comedy, he keeps right on falling, through one floor after another, right down to the basement. See *Kazaam, The Frighteners, Assassins,* etc. It's amazing such shaky buildings can stand up well enough for the characters to walk upstairs in the first place. (Note: These scenes, which are incredibly expensive, are never funny.)

R. E.

Inevitable Girl Next Door. In any movie where the hero is caught in a love triangle with two women, he will always choose the sweet, ordinary, caring one he grew up with—instead of the fabulously wealthy and gorgeous one with no morals. See *Cocktail, Teen Wolf.*

JEFF CROSS, Marblehead, Mass.

Inevitable Microfiche Library Scene. A tired visual cliché frequent in mystery thrillers, typically rendered in shot/reverse shot fashion: first shot: an intense close-up of the whirring blur of the microfiche view screen that suddenly locks onto a crystal-clear picture or article; second shot: the face of the shocked protagonist—suspicions confirmed! See *Sliver,* with Sharon Stone watching the whirring microfiche, until it locks onto the photo of the sliver building used throughout. Cut to: her stunned reaction.

DAVID H. COLEMAN, Tarzana, Calif.

Inevitable Sister. In any movie where the heroine catches her boyfriend dancing in public with another woman, and makes a big scene, the other woman invariably turns out to be the boyfriend's sister. See *Mystic Pizza,* etc.

STUART CLELAND, Chicago

Info-on-Demand. Whatever event the character is concerned or worried about (the killer on the loose, the police manhunt, the unusual disk-shaped lights in the sky, etc.), when the character turns on the radio or TV, there is an immediate news bulletin that provides full details of the event in question.

MIKE BACHERT, *Columbus, Ohio*

Ingenue Nudity Rule. In a movie with several young, pretty females, the prettiest among them, with the best body, will be the only one not seen nude.

DAVID STEVENS, *Irving, Tex.*

In-House Programming Syndrome. Movie characters only see movies in old-fashioned, single-auditorium movie houses and usually attend only revivals of old classics, or movies by the director of the one you're watching.

MERWYN GROTE, *St. Louis*

Injection Wince Reflex. Collective audience response whenever a large hypodermic syringe is used on a character in a movie. See *Pulp Fiction, Drugstore Cowboy, Rush, Alien 3*, etc.

WILLIAM BRANTLEY, *Paris, France*

Injured Reserve. Film athletes are never significantly injured during the course of the movie, unless the injury is the point of the story.

BRANNON MOORE, *Seattle*

In Space, No One Can Hear You Fall. Going through an airlock also causes one to become weightless.

NEIL MILSTED, Chicago

In Space, No One Can See You Scream. All space characters have bright lights installed in their helmets, pointing inward, so that we can better see their little faces. The fact that this would make them completely blind in the darkness of space is of no consequence.

FRED DECKER, Cary, N.C.

Instant Dye Job. Anybody in an action film entering a scene dressed entirely or mostly in white will by scene's end be splattered with bright red blood.

MICHAEL SCHLESINGER, Culver City, Calif.

Instant Ignition Rule. In an action movie, any car driven by bad guys that crashes will inevitably explode, with flames instantly filling the passenger compartment, just as though they were carrying open cans of gasoline in their laps. This also happens whenever a car occupied by bad guys begins to fall over a cliff, even before the car has hit anything.

SAM WAAS, Houston

Instant Ignition Syndrome. Whenever a character in a movie steps into a car, the keys are obviously in the ignition, judging by the lack of time required from when the door slams to when the car pulls into traffic. In some movies, one might assume that the car was left running. No one ever fumbles for keys, no one ever has to do the "pump twice and pray" thing, no matter how old or battered the car is. (Exception: "Hollywood Car Rule.")

DAWSON RAMBO, *Tucson, Ariz.*

Instant Wardrobe Rule. Anyone arriving in town without luggage–for example, a western hero riding into town with only his saddlebags–reappears immediately with a full change of clothes.

PATRICK HALL, *East Kilbride, Scotland*

Intelligence. In most movies, "all that separates us from the apes." In *Sheena, Queen of the Jungle,* what we have in common with them.

R. E.

Intelligent Universal Operating Systems. All computers in the movies use the same amazingly powerful operating system that accepts plain English commands. A character simply types OPEN PRIMARY FILE or ACCESS SECURITY SYSTEM. The computer immediately responds. Such computers are always connected to a massive global network, and can access any private file anywhere in the world. In addition, this operating system uses a gigantic, blocky font that is usually bright green on a black background, apparently for the benefit of visually impaired users.

JIM COLLIER, *Dallas*

Intense Directional Singing Voice. When there's a panning shot of a crowd singing, you hear a mushy blend of voices until the camera spots a lead actor; then you hear the lead's voice loud and clear.

CHRIS JONES, *Snellville, Ga.*

In the Nick of Heroism. Bad guy corners victim and points his gun. A shot rings out. Bad guy smiles ironically, then slumps to the ground, dead. Audience and victim realize at same time that victim is still alive. Someone else shot the bad guy in the back. Who? Camera cuts to the unlikely shooter/hero, a nonviolent type who was not supposed to be at the scene and has never fired a gun before. He or she is still aiming the gun, in trembling outstretched hand.

AMY NOVIT, *Melrose, Mass.*

Inverse Law of Combat Intensity. The intensity of combat in battle scenes is in inverse proportion to distance from the camera. The guys in the foreground usually at least *try* to look like they *may* want to hurt each other, but if you look in the far background you'll see "combatants" just kind of fanning each other with their swords. Extremely popular in, but not limited to, all Italian "sword and sandal" movies.

CHARLIE AMBROSI

Invisible Ceiling. Anyone can climb to the ceiling of a warehouse or practically anything else and not be seen by anyone walking beneath. In a subset of the "Fallacy of the Predictable Tree," if the good guy is hiding on or in the ceiling, the bad guy will pause directly underneath so the good guy can fall on him and overpower him. See *Sneakers.*

DONA KIGHT, *Chicago*

Invisible Protective Shield. Protects characters during fight scenes. They get hit by fists, chairs, bottles, etc., and thrown through walls, doors, glass, but wear only a small bandage in next scene, and later have no marks, although they should be black and blue for the rest of the movie.

CATHERINE WENT

It Just Might Work Rule. It always does, however—although not necessarily in the intended manner.

BRANNON MOORE, Seattle

It's a Black Thing Maneuver. Used when hero needs help or information, and has been refused by rigid bureaucracy. Just as he's leaving in defeat, he is called aside by an employee of the place who is of the same race/nationality/age/ethnicity as the hero, and who breaks the rules by quietly telling him what he needs to know.

MICHAEL E. ISBELL

"It's Over." Whenever a man and woman have narrowly escaped a series of deadly events, the man inevitably says to the woman, "It's over." She then nods gratefully. See *Seeing-Eye Man.*

MICHAEL J. PILLING, Maple Ridge, B.C., Canada

"I've got it on tape!" This line is always followed by the chipmunklike sound of a Stone Age tape recorder rewinding. The tape inevitably rewinds to the exact spot required to give only the pertinent portion of the incriminating statement, no matter how long the villain talked.

DON HOWARD, San Jose, Calif.

James T. Kirk Loophole. Any contrived plot twist that undoes the un-undoable. The JTK Loophole is named in the spirit of the *Star Trek* character who says, "I don't believe in a no-win situation"; thus, when Spock dies at the end of *Star Trek II,* he is resurrected in *Star Trek III.* Also, when Superman is told he can never turn back time, he does it anyway, and in *Superman II,* when he gives up his powers forever, he gets them back by the end of the movie. In *All Dogs Go to Heaven,* when the canine lead is told that if he leaves heaven he can never return, he does so with no questions asked. In *What Dreams May Come,* Robin Williams is told he can never get his wife out of hell, but does.

Merwyn Grote, St. Louis

Jarring Door Ajar Scene. In an action thriller, whenever the hero knocks on a door and it swings gently inward at the first tap, there is inevitably a dead body inside, often that of a close friend or an old law enforcement partner.

Mark and Sonya Warner, Le Creusot, France

Joel Silver Rule. All women in action-adventure flicks are extraneous to the plot unless naked or dead.

Jim O'Brien

Joel's Observation. Directors always make sure that air ducts are big enough to crawl around in.

First noted by Joel Robinson of
"Mystery Science Theater 3000"

Joint Forces Law. If two groups are fighting one another, and a third group comes in against the good guy's group, the original enemies of the good guy will join forces with him to combat against the third and most evil group. See *Rumble in the Bronx.*

RHYS SOUTHAN, *Richardson, Tex.*

Jolly Bornday. Any obviously concocted song sung during a birthday party scene, chosen so the producers can avoid paying the royalty fees for "Happy Birthday."

ANDY IHNATKO, *Westwood, Mass.*

Joy of Ex. If a cop's daughter or wife is seen in the first twenty minutes of a film, she will be either dead or kidnapped within the next hour. Corollary: If the wife is estranged, her safety is assured; by Hollywood law, the movie cannot end until the cop rescues her and they realize that Maybe They Belong Together After All.

ANDY IHNATKO, *Westwood, Mass.*

Jukebox Jerrybuilding. Movie based on a song solely to cash in on the popularity of the song. See *White Christmas, Chattanooga Choo-choo, Ode to Billy Joe, Harper Valley PTA, Girls Just Want to Have Fun, Sgt. Pepper's Lonely Hearts Club Band,* etc.

MERWYN GROTE, *St. Louis*

Jukebox Saturday Night Fights. Every time a fight breaks out in a bar, the jukebox volume goes way up. At the end of the fight, it goes right back down! Wow. What a trick! And the jukebox never plays a slow song during a brawl.

JOSHUA RASIEL, *West Nyack, N.Y.*

Ka-Ching! Moment. Instant when you realize the product on screen is a product placement and not just a prop; i.e., when the product stops being used by the film and the film starts being used by the product. When characters eat at McDonald's in *Ordinary People,* that's a movie; when they go to McDonald's in *MAC and Me* to party with Ronald McDonald, that's a commercial. When Michael J. Fox orders a Pepsi Free in *Back to the Future,* the soft drink is a prop. But when Bill Cosby spends an entire scene in *Leonard Part 6* holding a bottle of Coca-Cola so that the label is dead-center on camera, that is a product placement. (Tip off: When the product is more carefully lit than the actors are, like the Wheaties box on Superman's breakfast table.)

MERWYN GROTE, *St. Louis*

Keep Refrigerated until Ready to Barf. Coroners and morgue attendants always keep their lunch in the same refrigerator as the pickled body parts.

ROBERT HUTTON, *Bedminster, N.J.*

Kevin Kline Mustache Principle. When Kevin Kline is sporting facial hair he must play an eccentric, offbeat goofball *(A Fish Called Wanda, I Love You to Death, Soapdish).* To play a serious role he must be clean-shaven *(Dave, Sophie's Choice, Grand Canyon, Cry Freedom).*

ERIC SKOVAN, *Poughkeepsie, N.Y.*

103

Keyless Vehicle Exception. Just as the warehouse, oil refinery, or ammunition dump starts to explode, the hero dashes through a hail of burning debris, finds a truck, car, or motorcycle parked outside, throws it into gear, and roars away to safety.

ED COHEN, *Chicago*

Kidding Battery. In horror films, when the hero/heroine jumps in a car while being pursued by the killer, the car never starts at the first crank. The following generic montage is used: Close-up shot of hero/heroine's face sweating. Face goes out of focus as background focuses to reveal killer approaching car. Close-up of ignition failing again to start engine. Repeat sequence as many times as necessary to match generic crescendo music. Finally, battery gives enough juice to start engine just a second before killer gets the would-be victim. Obviously, the battery was just kidding.

RAYMOND SALFITI

Killer Imperative. Any character who voices a moral objection to killing, or who claims to have never before killed anyone, will be invariably called upon to do so (usually during the final third of the movie). The character either liquidates an imposing villain at very close range in self-defense, kills a bad guy a split second before he would have murdered the hero, or just "gets mad."

G. W. ROLES, *Washington, D.C.*

Kinetic Energy Amplification Phenomenon. In scenes involving gunplay, the kinetic energy of the bullets will be enormously amplified as they strike the victim, enabling him to be hurled great distances and through objects. This phenomenon is particularly common around windows and balconies, especially in high-rise buildings.

DENNIS WARD

Kinetic Energy Distortion Phenomenon. When someone is shot while standing near a window, balcony, or ledge, the kinetic energy will always be distorted so as to throw him *outward,* regardless of the direction the bullets came from. This enables victims to be hurled out a window and into a spectacular plunge even if the shots came from outside to begin with.

DENNIS WARD

Kirk Method of Time Management. Regardless of the time a subordinate says will be needed to fix a problem, the supervisor will cut the time by half, at least. Example: Scotty: "I'll need at least twenty minutes to repair the warp drive, Captain!" Captain Kirk: "You've got exactly ten minutes before the *Enterprise* is pulled into the Sun, Mr. Scott!"

ROBERT JONES, *Tigard, Oreg.*

Kojak Moment. In thrillers where the hero is befuddled by an assortment of completely unrelated suspects and victims, the scene in which he suddenly discovers a vacation photo of all of them in a big, grinning group pose.

ANDY IHNATKO, *Westwood, Mass.*

Kookalouris. Name for a large sheet of cardboard or plywood with holes in it, which is moved back and forth in front of a light to illuminate a character's face with moving light patterns. Popular in the 1930s; back in style again with the movies of Steven Spielberg, who uses a kookalouris with underlighting to show faces that seem to be illuminated by reflections from pots of gold, buckets of diamonds, pools of fire, pirate maps, and radioactive kidneys.

R. E.

Lambada Factor. No matter how quickly it gets made, any film produced to cash in on the latest fashion, fad, trend, or gimmick will be out of date by the time it is released because the fashion, fad, trend, or gimmick will have become passé. See break dancing, disco, macarena, etc.

MERWYN GROTE, *St. Louis*

Land Boom Rule. In any movie where there is a cocktail party featuring a chart, map, or model of a new real-estate development, a wealthy property developer will be found dead inside an expensive automobile.

R. E.

Last Cell Syndrome. Whenever a character must visit someone in jail, the jailed character's cell is always the last one on the cell block, so the visitor must slowly pass by every other cell in terror.

NEIL GABRIELE, *Nashville, Tenn.*

Last Grab Rule. People pushed off balconies always hang on to the balcony or the person who pushed them for a few seconds before inevitably plunging to their death. Their clutching hand is always pictured in a close-up. (Used twice in *Poison Ivy*.)

SCOTT DALZIEL

Last Match Theory. An almost-empty box of matches is never shown in a movie unless a shortage of matches will prove integral to the plot at some point. See *The Fifth Element*.

ROBERT UNDERWOOD, *Denver*

Last Try Law. After a character gives up on something, especially starting a car in an urgent situation, it will work on the last try, just in time. See *Ace Ventura, Back to the Future*.

RHYS SOUTHAN, *Richardson, Tex.*

Latino Laughers. In all action movies set in Mexico, sooner or later a gang of tough guys will corner the hero and laugh at him in unison while using the word "gringo."

R. E.

Laugh or Be Laughed Rule. When a villain who is the head of a band of wrongdoers laughs, everyone else laughs with him, or he gets angry and kills the nonlaugher. The exception is when the villain laughs but does not want his followers to laugh; in this case, he kills the person who does laugh. Wise gang members think before responding. See *No Escape, Batman*.

RHYS SOUTHAN, *Richardson, Tex.*

Lawn Dwarf Rule. Garden gnomes in movies exist solely for the purpose of being stolen by wacky protagonists. See *Box of Moonlight, The Full Monty, SubUrbia.*

ED SLOTA, *Warwick, R.I.*

Law of Canine/Feline Superperception. Household pets can unerringly detect and react to the presence of ghosts, aliens, or other nonhuman entities. Their warnings are invariably ignored.

DEREK WOOD, *Palo Alto, Calif.*

Law of Colorful Chemicals. In scenes set in any kind of laboratory, there are always lots of flasks filled with lots of bright, colorful chemicals—red, blue, green—when in reality virtually everything in most research labs is either clear or some shade of yellow. I can count on one hand the number of organic chemicals that are bright blue or green. The chemicals are invariably in glassware jammed together backward and sideways, in what the set designer thought was a neat-looking combination. See the Nicholson-Karloff quickie *The Terror,* where in the witch's room we see a modern ground-glass three-neck flask, with the logo of the glass company clearly visible on its side. This during the Napoleonic wars.

DEREK LOWE, *Scotch Plains, N.J.*

Law of Economy of Characters. Movie budgets make it impossible for any film to contain unnecessary characters. Therefore, all characters in a movie are necessary to the story—even those who do not seem to be. Sophisticated viewers can use this law to deduce the identity of a person being kept secret by the movie's plot: This "mystery" person is always the only character in the movie who seems otherwise extraneous. (Cf. the friendly neighbor in *The Lady in White;* see also "Unmotivated Close-up.")

R. E.

Law of Economy of Instruction. Nobody is ever taught anything in a movie that he or she is not later called upon to use.

R. E.

Law of Fate Law. If a man and a woman meet, and the woman's husband has disappeared, the man and the woman will fall in love, and then the husband will suddenly reappear. See *Wife of Martin Guerre, Lord of Illusions.*

RHYS SOUTHAN, *Richardson, Tex.*

Law of Inevitable Immersion. Whenever characters are near a body of water, the chances are great that one of them will jump, fall, or be pushed into it. If this does occur, it is inevitable that the other character(s) will also jump, fall, or be pushed in. See *Sullivan's Travels* (swimming pool), *La Dolce Vita* (Roman fountain), *Tom Jones* (pond), *A Room with a View* (rural stream), *Summertime* (Grand Canal), etc.

STUART CLELAND, *Chicago*

Law of Inverse Wariness. The more dangerous the prisoner, the more lax the security precautions.

JEFF LEVIN, *Rochester, N.Y.*

Law of Inevitable Immersion

Law of Movie Brand Loyalty. Thanks to product placement, all characters in a movie, no matter how heterogeneous or geographically dispersed, drink one brand of beer, use one brand of sporting equipment, drive cars produced by one company, etc.

PAUL A. LEE, Germantown, Wis.

Law of Poignant Remnants. Whenever the wreckage of a plane crash is shown, there is always a teddy bear or doll in the midst of the wreckage.

NAOKI SATO, University of Toronto

Law of Relative Walking Speeds. No matter how fast the would-be victim runs, the slasher can always keep up just by walking steadily.

R. E.

Law of Take-out Chinese Food. Take-out Chinese food is eaten in one of only two situations: Communally by a large, multiethnic group enthusiastically working on a common project *(Reversal of Fortune),* or in bed by two post-coital lovers *(Annie Hall).* In the former case, the meal predicts success; in the latter, that the couple will break up.

PHILLIP L. GIANOS, Fullerton, Calif.

Law of Video Box Caricature, The. If you're trying to pick out a video and the actors on the box are cartooned caricatures which are not recognizable, pick another movie.

MARK BREWER, Lake Zurich, Ill.

Law of Vinyl Vulnerability. Unwritten rule in older Hollywood movies which decrees that any LP "vinyl" record album shown playing on a turntable must either be roughly grabbed and smashed to bits by a sad, depressed, or angry character who hates the song, or the tone arm needle must be violently dragged across its surface, thus ruining the record, in order to instantly hush a loud, annoying, and insensitive party crowd—whereupon the sad, depressed, or angry character demands in a loud voice that everybody must leave now.

ROBERT E. HUNT JR.

Lawyer with One Case Scenario. In nearly all legal dramas, the lawyers involved have only one case—the case that the movie is about. They are never distracted by other cases, clients, or causes.

MARTIN J. KEENAN, ESQ., *Great Bend, Kans.*

Lazenby Factor. Tendency of actors plucked from obscurity for a once-in-a-lifetime role to be just as quickly drop-kicked back into obscurity. Victims include George Lazenby of *On Her Majesty's Secret Service,* Klinton Spilsbury of *The Legend of the Lone Ranger,* Mark Lester of *Oliver!,* Kim Darby of *True Grit,* Bo Derek of *10,* Harold Russell of *The Best Years of Our Lives,* Haing S. Ngor of *The Killing Fields,* Maria Schneider of *Last Tango in Paris,* George Chakiris of *West Side Story,* Loren Dean of *Billy Bathgate,* Jaye Davidson of *The Crying Game.*

MERWYN GROTE, *St. Louis*

Leaky Specimen Tank Phenomenon. In all films dealing with science, whenever a big glass tube is displayed, there is a small column of bubbles rising to the surface. These bubbles, which might indicate to a scientist that there was a small hole in the bottom of the tube, are employed to prove to the audience that the container holds fluid, and to add atmosphere.

TOM ELBERFELD, *Chicago*

Leap in Timers. Stuntmen posing as pedestrians, who jump out of the way of speeding carts at the last moment, by leaping to fire escape ladders or off the sides of bridges.

MERWYN GROTE, *St. Louis*

Left Behind Rule. All Italian-American cops have a childhood friend who's in the Mafia.

IAN MANTGANI, *Liverpool, England*

Lenny Rule. Named for the gentle giant in Steinbeck's *Of Mice and Men,* this rule dictates that if a film character is of less than normal intelligence or ability, he or she will inadvertently get into serious trouble during the film.

STUART CLELAND, *Chicago*

Leno Device. Assures us the events in a movie received national attention by the appearance of Jay Leno on television, who makes a joke about it. Required particularly in political comedies. See *Wag the Dog, Dave, The Birdcage, Contact, Mad City.*

JASON BAILEY, *Wichita, Kans.*

Less-Is-More Rule. The less a preview shows, the more confidence the filmmakers have in their film and the more eager they are to let the audience be surprised. (If the trailer seems to tell the entire story of a film, it probably does; there is likely no reason to see the film.)

MERWYN GROTE, *St. Louis*

Letter Imperfect Law. If the opening credits are spelled out in a mismatched mixture of fonts and sizes designed to say "wacky," the movie is already in serious trouble.

MERWYN GROTE, *St. Louis*

Let Your Fingers Do the Crawling. Governors always wait until the last possible moment to put through a call with a stay of execution. No matter how long they have had to ponder the merits of the case, they never pick up the phone until the intended victim is strapped in the chair and the warden's fingers are tapping on the power switch.

R. E.

Let Your Fingers Do the Driving. In any movie where the hero knows that other characters are in trouble, say because a time bomb is about to go off, he must jump into a car and drive like a lunatic across town to save them. No hero ever has a quarter for the pay phone.

BILL BECWAR, *Wauwatosa, Wis.*

Libertyvalance. Verb, meaning to rewrite the facts of a story to match the storyteller's personal hero-worshiping impulses or make the tale more commercial. Drawn from John Ford's 1962 classic Western *The Man Who Shot Liberty Valance,* which had the moral "When the legend becomes fact, print the legend!" Examples of conversational usage: "D. W. Griffith really libertyvalanced the Ku Klux Klan in *The Birth of a Nation,* in order to make the story more compelling." Or "Oliver Stone's libertyvalancing in *JFK* reached epic proportions." Or "The libertyvalancization of *Gandhi* won Attenborough an Oscar!" Or "Disney found Pocahontas quite libertyvalanceable." Generally speaking, the more a filmmaker defends the honesty of his work, the more likely he is a libertyvalancer.

MERWYN GROTE, St. Louis

Light Fantasic, The. Curious set design principle that requires malfunctioning computer equipment to be accompanied by purposeless, flashing light displays.

PAUL A. LEE, Germantown, Wis.

Lightning-Thunder-Downpour. In most suburban and rural thrillers involving a vulnerable heroine, a bolt of lightning, then thunder, and then an instantaneous downpour of hard rainfall occurs in rapid sequence, with no rumblings or darkened skies as forewarning. (The "Wet Road Rule" inevitably applies here.)

STEVE W. ZACK

Limited Partnership. If a young up-and-coming actor is playing the hero's partner, said partner will be killed *(In the Line of Fire, Copycat).* If the hero is the up-and-comer, then his mentor, played by a veteran actor, will buy it *(Star Wars, The Untouchables,* and *The Mask of Zorro).* Full stardom is when an actor plays only roles that fall between these two career stages.

CHRISTOPHER M. TERRY, *Atlanta, Ga.*

Limo Exclusion Law. In any scene involving a limousine, where one actor is in the back seat talking to another actor outside the car, the scene will end with the actor in the car raising the window, reflecting back onto the outside actor the world he's stuck in.

MARK ORISTANO

Little Man Big Man Rule. Whenever one character is tall and the other is short and plump, the short one is always the brains and the tall one is the dummy. See *Home Alone,* etc.

DAVID ORMESHER, *Lakeland, Fla.*

Locked in Low. A good sprinter can run the 100-yard dash in ten seconds. That's twenty miles an hour. Yet overweight, out-of-shape heroes can run down the center of the road when fleeing bad guys' cars, and the cars never catch them. That's because the cars are Locked in Low and can't do more than ten miles an hour.

DON HOWARD, *San Jose, Calif.*

Long-Haired Woman Seen from Behind. When approached by hero, inevitably turns out to be a man.

R. E.

Looney In-Tunes. Any movie with a plot about a success-ful musician returning to his hometown for any reason will feature a scene where he or she picks up his "first" in-strument or sits in front of his grandmother's piano. Of course this instrument is in tune.

PATTY SUNDBERG, *Tucson, Ariz.*

Love Boat Rule. Any character who coughs at any time has a terminal illness. Happens all the time on "The Love Boat," oddly enough. See *Camille*.

JAMES R. JOKERST, *Maryland*

Love-Hate Principle. Any attractive man and woman who hate each other at the beginning of a movie will be in love at the end.

CHARLES D. STORY, *Elmhurst, Ill.*

Lucky Pedestrians. No matter how many trash cans, water hydrants, fruit carts, or other cars get hit during a car chase or by a runaway auto, pedestrians are safe from harm. The rationale is simple. Hit a pedestrian, and that would distract from the mindless action.

MERWYN GROTE, *St. Louis*

Mabel, the AT&T Phone. The AT&T telephones used in the movies are like standard models, except that the AT&T logo (known to company insiders as the Death Star) is printed on the heel of the handset, so that when an actor is speaking on the phone, it is clearly visible. AT&T makes no phones like this in real life. For numerous

Love-Hate Principle

Mabel sightings, see *The Fugitive*. Mabel is never used in scenes calling for someone to be bashed to death with a telephone.

RICH ELIAS, *Delaware, Ohio*

Ma Bell Rule. Whenever a telephone is seen in a movie, the telephone will eventually ring.

KEN COX, *Florence, S.C.*

MacGuffin. Alfred Hitchcock's term for a plot element that "must seem to be of vital importance to the characters," even though its specific identify is immaterial. "It's the device, the gimmick, if you will, or the papers the spies are after," Hitchcock explained to François Truffaut in their book-length interview. Hitchcock illustrated with the story of two hunters in the Scottish Highlands. One asks the other what is in his package. "A MacGuffin," the other responds. "What's a MacGuffin?" "It's an apparatus for trapping lions." "But there are no lions in the High-lands." "Then that's not a MacGuffin!" See also "O'Guffin."

R. E.

MacLaine's Law of Female Fatality. If a movie features three female leads, one of them will die during childbirth. If there are five or more female leads, an additional female character will contract a terminal disease.

ANDY IHNATKO, Westwood, Mass.

Mad Dash into Traffic Rule. A car will always brake close enough for the running hero to touch it, and then dash into the next lane where the same thing happens with a car traveling in the opposite direction.

BARAK and ELIZABETH MOORE, Jerusalem, Israel

Mad Slasher Movies. Movies starring a mad-dog killer who runs amok, slashing all of the other characters. The killer is frequently masked (as in *Halloween* and *Friday the 13th*), not because a serious actor would be ashamed to be seen in the role, but because then no actor at all is required; the only skills necessary are the ability to wear a mask and wield a machete. For additional reading, see *Splatter Movies,* by John ("Mutilation is the Message") McCarty.

R. E.

Magical Death Hand Wave. When a relative or partner of the hero is murdered, and the hero must view the body, always still at the scene of the crime, the hero will pass his hand over the eyes of the victim, and (voilà!) magically, the eyes will remain closed.

DAWSON RAMBO, *Tucson, Ariz.*

Magical Death Hand Wave

Magical Makeup Syndrome. Women in old romantic films never take off their makeup, even in the bath, and certainly not in bed. Their elaborate hairdos are as rigid as corrugated iron. When they cry, their eyes run, but never their noses, and definitely never their mascara. Their fingernails and toenails never have chipped nail

Magical Makeup Syndrome

polish, and they look immaculate even if they have just been dragged through a coal chute by the hair.

HILARY POTTS, West Ealing, London

Magic Bullets. If someone is firing a machine gun at someone's upper body, any bullets that do not hit them will make a 90-degree turn in the plane of their body and kick up dust at their feet.

BRANNON MOORE, Seattle

Magic Bus. During a chase on foot, if a bus or any other vehicle longer than a van comes between the chaser and the chasee, the person being chased will magically disappear, thus leaving the chaser dumbfounded.

CHRISTOPHER I. HENRY, Ann Arbor, Mich.

Magic Shave. When a shaving actor is interrupted after just a few strokes, he wipes the lather off with a towel to reveal a close-shaved face.

PATRICK HALL, East Kilbride, Scotland

Magnetic Beach Effect. Whenever a storm at sea capsizes boats and leaves the shipwreck survivors adrift and helpless, the next dawn finds them sprawled on a beach. It is always a nice, clear day.

R. E.

Maid to Die Dictum. In a thriller, if a housemaid or baby-sitter is seen early in the film as part of the family unit, and is given an identity but virtually no dialogue, she will be killed when the villain shows up. The movie will never mention her death again.

MERWYN GROTE, St. Louis

Ma Jarrett Rule. Behind every good villain who wears a balaclava for heists, there is a caring mom who sews up the frayed edges once the holes have been cut for his eyes and mouth.

SUE FEEHAN, Beckenham, Kent, England

Make/Up Rule. A movie baby will inevitable "make" on anyone who picks it up. ("What a cute baby! What th . . . ? Ugh!")

PHILIP LEW, Brooklyn, N.Y.

Making that Last Sale. In the case of any impending disaster, natural or man-made, politicians will always arrive at the same conclusion: It is less important to issue a warning than to "avoid panicking the population." The reasoning is always the same: A warning will be bad for business.

EUGENE ACCARDO, Brooklyn

Mamet Dammit. Variations of the "f-word" packaged in multiples *and* shoehorned into banal dialogue to establish gritty reality. Prolific users of the Mamet Dammit include Martin Scorsese, Brian DePalma, Paul Schrader, John Milius, Quentin Tarantino, and David Mamet. If you are aware of the profanity (like in *Scarface, Glengarry Glen Ross,* or *Reservoir Dogs*) it is the Mamet Dammit; if at the end of the movie you don't remember there being any profanity *(Rain Man)*, it isn't.

MERWYN GROTE, St. Louis

Mandatory Latrine Scene. In movies since 1980 with office settings, all major decisions are made by men of power while standing next to urinals and washbasins in the men's restroom.

DONNA MARTIN, Kansas City, Mo.

Mano y Ammo. Scene in action movie where hero outfits himself with every form of weaponry he can possibly carry. The scene is usually choreographed with crisp movements and involves more zippers and Velcro than a Michael Jackson concert.

JOHN WILLARD, Cortez, Colo.

Marathon Hero, The. A hero in pursuit of a purse-snatcher or getaway car can run for many blocks, even up the hills of San Francisco, without getting winded.

R. E.

Martini Shot. In a production schedule, the last shot of principal photography at the end of the day is called the "Martini Shot," after which the crew can retire for the day and, in theory, enjoy a martini.

SAM HUMPHRIES

Meet Cute. Time-honored Hollywood method of having two important characters meet each other. In the Golden Age, it often involved the heroine exiting from a department store and dropping her packages after being jostled by the hero. As they stoop to pick them up, their heads bump, leading to conversation, etc. In modern movies, Meet Cutes can be more ingenious. In *With Honors,* for example, a Harvard student meets a homeless man after a thesis falls through a sidewalk grating.

R. E.

Method Nose Acting. As a continual visual reminder that a character is self-destructive and has lost his dignity, the story will call for him to injure his nose, requiring him to walk around wearing a nose bandage. Examples: Jack Nicholson in *Chinatown,* Patrick Stewart in *Conspiracy Theory,* Sylvester Stallone in *Cop Land,* etc.

MARK DAYTON, Cosa Mesa, Calif.

Mid-Wife Crisis. Any character whose wife and/or kids are introduced more than an hour into the movie and who hugs and kisses any or all of them will be dead within the next twenty minutes (e.g., "Goose" in *Top Gun*).

EDWARD SAVIO, San Francisco

Milli-Vanilli Props. Novelty gadgets available today, but used in sci-fi/fantasy movies as futuristic devices. For example, in *Star Trek III: The Search For Spock,* McCoy is in a *Star Wars*–type bar with lava lamps.

TERRY FOX

Miracle of Available Parking Space. When a character needs a parking space, even on the busiest streets in the busiest cities, one is quickly found. For example, in *Lost*

Milli-Vanilli Props

in America, Albert Brooks finds space for a Winnebago directly in front of an office building at midday in New York City. Corollary: When a character needs to pull into traffic, there is always a break.

PHILLIP L. GIANOS, *Fullerton, Calif.*

Miracle Twenty-five-pound Newborn Syndrome. Newborn babies in movies instantly look about seven months old, and weigh about twenty-five pounds. Their postpartum mother seems perfectly refreshed, made-up, and comfortable despite the gargantuan child she's just given birth to.

BARAK and ELIZABETH MOORE, *Jerusalem, Israel*

Miraculous Projection Phenomenon. Ability of apparently normal computer, TV, and movie screens to project their images onto the face of an actor. In extreme cases, the audience is able the read the crisply focused words from a computer screen directly off an actor's face.

RICHARD ROHRDANZ, *West Kennebunk, Maine*

Mirror Gimmick. Tired old cinemagraphic trick in which we think we are seeing a character, but then the camera pans and we realize we were only looking in a mirror.

ARDEN J. COOPER, *Warren, Mich.*

Mirror Gimmick II. We see the hero in serious conversation (trying to propose marriage, for example). After a few lines the camera pans back and we realize he was only rehearsing his speech. See *Forever Young.*

LAUREL VAN DYKE, *Kokomo, Ind.*

"Miss Blanche?" Character. Any character in a film who is a false hero and exists only to get killed for shock value—usually seconds after they've found out the villain. Examples: Detective Arbogast in *Psycho,* the cop in *Misery,* the brother in *The Stepfather,* the football player in the remake of *The Blob,* and, of course, the maid in *Whatever Happened to Baby Jane?* (The name comes from her last words.)

ROB MATSUSHITA, *Madison, Wis.*

Mission Control Syndrome. Tired but insidious device in which filmmaker prompts the audience to react after failing to explain why anyone should care. The action is intercut with footage of a contrived surrogate audience, reacting with mounting tension—and then ecstatic, arm-waving, paper-hurling jubilation. Easy in sports movies; overlabored in films like *WarGames* (spurious Pentagon war room), *The Right Stuff* (mission control), all the *Airport* movies (control tower), *The Hunt for Red October* (Pentagon again). Most end-of-the-world movies have an obligatory roomful of scientists to monitor approaching doom.

ANGUS MCCALLUM, *New York City*

Modesty Maneuver. Movie characters are so self-effacing that whenever they perform extravagantly dangerous acts, they keep their backs to the cameras. This is followed by a close-up of the character, signifying that the stuntman has done his job and the actor is back at work.

MERWYN GROTE, *St. Louis*

Moe Rule of Bomb Disposal. Used by bomb squad experts in movies. When they know that cutting one wire will deactivate the bomb and cutting the other will make it explode, the correct wire to cut is always "Moe." All movie bomb experts clamp their cutters around one wire but end up cutting the other at the last moment. ("Eenie, meenie, minie . . . snip!")

ANDY IHNATKO, *Westwood, Mass.*

Monk's Reward. A surprising final line or image, tagged on after the credits have finished rolling (e.g., in *Airplane!*, the fellow in the taxicab at the airport, still yakking). So named because it usually takes monklike devotion to sit through the credits to get to it. (Also known as Credit Cookies.)

SERDOR YEGULALP

Monokini Law. All bikini-oriented movies, including swimsuit videos, are required by California law to have at least one scene where the top is removed for comic effect. Bonus points if done by a dog.

DAVID STEVENS, *Irving, Tex.*

Most Dangerous Road Syndrome. Any group of refugees walking along any road in France between 1940 and 1944 will be strafed by the Luftwaffe.

MATTHEW COPE, *Montreal*

Movie-Bismol. When characters in movies have indigestion, they never just take Rolaids. They always mix up some gross concoction of Alka-Seltzer or Pepto-Bismol with beer, booze, milk, and/or coffee. No one outside of a movie has ever done this. See *Courage Under Fire, Cape Fear,* etc.

JON PIETROWSKI, *Genoa, Ohio*

Movie Businesswoman Look. Whenever a high-powered businesswoman appears in a movie, her suit always includes a mini-length skirt and a low-cut blouse (and she always has great legs). If ordinary businesswomen dressed that way, they'd never be taken seriously, and in some companies they'd even be violating a dress policy (e.g., Demi Moore in *Disclosure*).

KAY ROBART, *Austin, Tex.*

Movie Dumb. Outrageously inaccurate information about filmmaking, in films about making films. Examples: In *Mrs. Doubtfire,* Robin Williams postdubs the voices to cartoons when it is common practice to record the voices first and match the animation to fit. In *Hooper,* a complicated stunt sequence is filmed in one continuous take. In *The Stuntman,* a man is recruited as a stuntman and placed in dangerous situations without getting training or even knowing exactly what the stunt involves. In *S.O.B.,* sets used in the movie-within-the-movie are still set up on a studio soundstage months later, after the finished film has already premiered and flopped. The plot of *Broadcast News* hinges on an experienced producer not realizing that a character has faked a reaction shot.

MERWYN GROTE, *St. Louis*

Movie Giftwrap Rule. When characters in movies receive wrapped presents, the lid is usually wrapped separately from the box—presumably so that if the scene has to be reshot, the gift can be "re-wrapped" quickly.

GEORGE M. IACONO, *Chicago*

Movieland, CA, and Filmtown, N.Y. The two towns which are the setting for all movies in which characters dial the phony numbers (408) 555–XXXX and (212) 555–XXXX. Any phone call made to these exchanges will connect you to a fabulous movie celebrity or extra!

ANDY IHNATKO, *Westwood, Mass.*

Movie Medicine Men. No disease is incurable for the elderly doctors or medicine men of third-world cultures, who always produce a secret powder or herb. The medicine's action is triggered by the simple poetic philosophy which accompanies the treatment.

R. E.

"Mr. Electricity Is Our Friend" Principle. The safety fence around a transformer or similar high-voltage equipment magically becomes charged when a bad guy is thrown against it, invariably with spectacular results. When the good guy hits the same fence earlier in the fight, nothing happens.

ERIC AMICK, Columbia, Md.

Mr. Magooser Interface. Computers in movies are often unable to display anything more than three lines of very large letters during normal operations. All the computers in the Star Trek films, for instance, sport the classic Magooser Interface; during a crisis, all screens clear themselves of useful information and display RED ALERT in jumbo letters, instead of informing the crew what exactly the problem is and how they might solve it.

ANDY IHNATKO, Westwood, Mass.

Multiple Death Requirement. In virtually all action films, the primary villain or antagonist in a film must be dispatched in more than one fashion. It is sufficient for minor characters to be killed by a solitary method (shot, stabbed, neck broken, dropped from a great height, maimed, burned, crushed, mauled, etc.), but the villain must be killed in several ways at once. There are dozens of examples of death by two means. The most common is for the villain to be fatally shot and then finished off by a more creative method, as in *Die Hard* (shot and dropped from a great height), *Fatal Attraction* (drowned and shot), *Indiana Jones and the Temple of Doom* (dropped from a great height and eaten by alligators), and *Goldeneye*

(dropped from a great height and crushed). Death by three simultaneous means is rare but not unheard of, as in *Rambo III* (dropped from a great height, neck broken, and blown up) and *The Last Boy Scout* (shot, dropped from a great height, and chopped to pieces by a helicopter's blades).

MARK KILLEFER, *Knoxville, Tenn.*

Murphy's Law. In movies made before 1985, any character named "Murphy" was a cop, a priest, a drunk, a tough guy, or all of the above. *Murphy's Romance* was the first to break with this rule. Prior to TV's Murphy Brown, all Murphys were male. Any character named Murphy will sooner or later be shown in a saloon, or drinking heavily.

ROBERT F. MURPHY, *Providence, R.I.*

Musician's Close-Up Rule. All quick cuts to nightclubs begin with a close-up of the drum being whacked. The camera then backs off the close-up of the whacking hands to reveal the full musician, the rest of the band, and finally the audience. See *Ed Wood, Batman Forever,* etc.

STEVEN SOUZA, *Honolulu, Hawaii*

Myopia Rule. Little girls who wear glasses in the movies always tell the truth. Little boys who wear glasses in the movies always lie.

GENE SISKEL

Myopic Visionary. In movies in which time travel or nostalgia takes us back to the 1940s or 1950s, the obligatory character who is loudly skeptical of the viability of television or Japanese industry announces he's about to go out and buy an Edsel.

ANDY IHNATKO, Westwood, Mass.

Mysterious Object Antecedents Myth. Whenever a movie involves time travel, there will always be an object that travels between the past and future without ever having actually come from anywhere. Example: In the beginning of *Somewhere in Time,* an old Jane Seymour gives the young Christopher Reeve a pocket watch. He travels back in time to find her, taking the watch with him, and accidentally leaves it there. She keeps it, grows old, and–voilà–the cycle repeats itself. But where did the pocket watch come from in the first place?

BARBARA KELSEY

Mystery Guest. At a crowded table, the sole empty chair and place setting, positioned right between the camera and the actors. Traditionally placed there in memory of L. B. Mayer, whose second coming was foretold by the prophet Winchell.

ANDY IHNATKO, Westwood, Mass.

Mystery of the Levitating Ghost. If the hero can jump through the wall of the moving subway train, why doesn't he fall through the floor?

BILL BECWAR, Wauwatosa, Wis.

Myth of the Seemingly Ordinary Day. The day begins like any other, with a man getting up, having breakfast, reading the paper, leaving the house, etc. His activities are so uneventful they are boring. That is the tip-off. No genuine ordinary day can be allowed to be boring in a movie. Only seemingly ordinary days—which inevitably lead up to a shocking scene of violence, which punctuates the seeming ordinariness.

R. E.

Nah Reflex. Character sees someone but can't believe his eyes, so shakes his head and says, "Nah." Inevitably it is the person it couldn't be.

JOHN WECKMUELLER, *Menomonie, Wis.*

Naked Truth. The more notorious the nude scene, the harder it will be to take the actor/actress doing it seriously as a performer. The more credible the actor/actress already is, the less notorious the nude scene will be.

MERWYN GROTE, *St. Louis*

National Geographic Rule. Full frontal nudity in foreign films is called art. In American movies, it's called pornography.

DAVID STEVENS, *Irving, Tex.*

Nazi Sentry Syndrome. Nazi soldiers on sentry duty invariably suffer from acute drowsiness. Their peripheral vision shrinks to the area directly in front of them, and they become hard of hearing. When attacked, their vocal chords can produce only muffled Teutonic grunts.

DAVID NEVARD, *Waltham, Mass.*

Near Miss Kiss. The hero and heroine are about to kiss. Their lips are a quarter of an inch apart—but then they're interrupted.

> Douglas W. Topham, *Woodland Hills, Calif.*

Necessity of the Elaborate Weapon. Any film containing a character who used to be an elite soldier of any kind will have him elect to use a weapon that looks like a reject from the *Star Wars* effects shop. There will be a scene where the hero assembles this weapon from a foam-lined aircraft-aluminum suitcase.

> Dawson Rambo, *Tucson, Ariz.*

Neckage Ploy. The marketing theory that large expanses of a woman's bare neck on a video box will give the impression that the movie contains eroticism, thereby causing it to be rented.

> David Stevens, *Irving, Tex.*

Neon Sign Rule. Whenever the leading male is hiding out or thrown out of his house by his wife and has to spend the night in a sleazy hotel, he always gets the room with the hotel's blinking neon sign right outside his window.

> Eugene Accardo, *Brooklyn, N.Y.*

Nerd Rule. In any teenager movie the nerd character will, by the end of the film, be dating the prettiest girl in the school, proving that nerds are people too.

> Lisa Martin, *Toronto*

New Tenant Rule. Large corporations are always situated in the flashiest, shiniest, tallest, most imposing, and architecturally dazzling buildings in town. Their names, however, always look like they were painted with poster paint on cardboard by an apprentice in the studio sign shop.

JOHN MAYER, *North Hollywood, Calif.*

Newton's Fourth Law. Heroes in movies who fall from great heights will land on shrubs, cardboard boxes, awnings, or something else that cushions their fall. Villains land on steel fence posts, or in the path of a speeding bus.

JEFFREY R. FIELD, *Kansas City, Mo.*

Newton's Laws Repealed. In which action becomes mysteriously decoupled from reaction, usually in connection with a firearm. Typically, a bullet from the hero's handgun lifts the villain off his feet and hurls him backward (often through one of those ubiquitous plate-glass windows that cars like to drive through) while the hero doesn't budge a millimeter. (Action equals reaction, right? The hero should be hurled backward with equal force.)

ROBERT J. LANG, *Altadena, Calif.*

Nicolas Cage Wig-Out Scene. No Nicolas Cage movie is complete without the scene in which Cage's character finally loses his temper and screams at the top of his lungs. The finest example is in *Red Rock West,* where he shouts "%*&! Mexico!" at Lara Flynn Boyle.

TOM CAMMALLERI, *Newbury Park, Calif.*

Nightmare Reflex. Character wakes from a nightmare by sitting bolt upright in a bed with bulging eyes and sweat all over his face.

FRASER SMITH, Tampa, Fla.

Niner Rule. Whenever a movie requires the use of military-style radio transmission (i.e., "Romeo Oscar Golf Echo Romeo" for "Roger"), if any numbers are being transmitted, one of them will always be "Niner," because it sounds so cool.

DAWSON RAMBO, Tucson, Ariz.

Nineteen RMS W/VU. Unless the point is to establish poverty, the apartments occupied by movie characters always look much larger and more expensive than anyone on their salary could afford. If the point is to establish "colorful" poverty, the occupants are so poor they can only afford to furnish with antiques.

R. E.

Noble Savage Syndrome. Thrown into the company of a native tribe of any description, the protagonist discovers the true meaning of life and sees through the sham of modern civilization. Wisdom and sensitivity are inevitably possessed by any race, class, age group, or ethnic or religious minority that has been misunderstood. Such movies seem well intentioned at first glance, but replace one stereotype for another; the natives seem noble, but never real. They may be starving, but if they're noble and have a few good songs, why worry?

ROBERT F. MURPHY

No Cigar Rule. No film with fewer than five nominated Academy Awards can win for Best Picture.

GERALD FITZGERALD, *Dallas*

No Corpus Delicti. If a movie begins with a murder and the body is never found, the supposed victim is not really dead and will pop up at the end, revealed as the perpetrator of all subsequent killings.

MICHAEL SCHLESINGER, *Culver City, Calif.*

No-Fail Pregnancy Predictor. Any woman of childbearing age in any movie who is ever nauseous.

BARAK and ELIZABETH MOORE, *Jerusalem, Israel*

Non-Answering Pet. In any horror or suspense movie, if the family pet does not come after being called at least twice by the protagonist or a member of his family, he is dead. This sometimes happens after he has served as an example of the Law of Canine/Feline Superperception (q.v.).

JOHN SHANNON

Nothing? Nothing Will Come of Nothing! If a character has something he finds hard to say, the dialogue will go like this: "John?" "Yeah?" (Brief pause.) "Nothing."

WILL GRIFFIN, *Bristol, England*

Nothing Says Loving Like a Dial Tone. Standard scene in romance: Romeo rushes out into dark and stormy night to a pay phone to call Juliet. He puts in quarter and dials. Juliet answers: "Hello? HELLO?" Romeo says nothing, and hangs up. Juliet hears the dial tone and stares at the receiver, wondering who it possibly could have been.

David Nemetz, New York, N.Y.

Not-So-Bad Bad Guy. He kills people, therefore, he is worse than the Good Bad Guy (q.v.). However, he is not a villain if he never kills women or children. He only kills their husbands, sons, brothers, or fathers, but nobody's perfect.

Alexis S. Mendez, Aguadilla, Puerto Rico

Nuns and Sailors Rule. Every single airport and train station waiting room in the movies contains both nuns and sailors.

Teresa Gregory, Indianapolis, Ind.

Obligatory M & M Shot. Every movie that features a scene in an Arab or Islamic country will begin the scene with a shot of a mosque tower (minaret), or the sound of the muezzin, or both.

Osamah Abdullatif, Muscat, Oman

Obligatory Nightgown Rule. Every adult woman getting out of bed in every movie will pick up a nightgown from the foot of the bed and put it on. Virtually no one can identify an instance of this happening in real life.

David Stevens, Irving, Tex.

Obligatory Transformational Entrance Scene. After being an ugly duckling for three-quarters of the movie, the heroine inevitably turns up at the top of a monumental staircase, looking breathtakingly beautiful and regal, and descends the stairs trying her best to keep one of those "are they looking at poor little me?" looks on her face.

R. E.

Obligatory Unrelated Opening Crisis. In any big-budget action movie, the spectacular title sequence never has anything to do with the rest of the story.

R. E.

Odd Couple Formula. Seemingly incompatible characters are linked to each other in a plot which depends on their differences for its comic and dramatic interest (c.f. *Tango and Cash, Homer and Eddie, Lethal Weapon, Loose Cannons*). Essential that one member of each team be a slob, as revealed by presence of fast-food wrappers in backseat of his Hollywood Cop Car (q.v.).

R. E.

Odd Information Clue. Bad exposition is often a give-away to plot points, since there must be a reason why we're getting all this otherwise inexplicable information. The most trivial fact delivered in the most offhand manner in Act I will prove monumentally significant, come denouement time.

JEFF LEVIN, *Rochester, N.Y.*

Odds on Edge Rule. The odds that a car in real life will be able to travel any appreciable distance balanced on two wheels: 1 in 7 million. The odds that this will happen during a chase scene in a movie: 1 in 43.

R. E.

Obligatory Transformational Entrance Scene

O'Guffin. Inspired by Hitchcock's MacGuffin (q.v.). A scene or sequence that has nothing to do with the plot of the film. Usually found lurking in B-movies, as an entertainment filler device, to mask the fact that the film has little or no actual story. See the Compulsory Topless Bar Scene in most R-rated cop action movies.

JIM and ROSE PFEIFER, *Southfield, Mich.*

Old Car Omen of Doom. Any best friend, suspect, informer, or witness who drives a car more than five years older than the cars owned by the rest of the characters in the film will be destroyed along with the car (via cliffs, explosions, etc.) before the film is over.

MERWYN GROTE, *St. Louis*

Omar the Folding Tentmaker. Whenever a movie hero is suddenly interrupted in the midst of a passionate sexual performance and is required to stand up (in undies or with a towel), he never reveals any physical evidence of his recent arousal.

JOHN STARR, *Glendale, Calif.*

Omens of War. (1) One man shows another a photo of his wife, kids, sweetheart, etc. This photo always reappears when the man is killed, to remind us of his warmth. (2) Man on guard duty says to comrade, "It's quiet." The laconic reply is always, "Yeah . . . too damn quiet!" (3) When seated around a fire on the eve of battle, a harmonica is often played by a young boy who later dies a hero's death. His body is later shown in close-up, harmonica still in hand.

MAX THOMPSON, *Kent, England*

142

Omnipresent Hydrant Rule. No car in a movie ever jumps over a curb without hitting a fire hydrant, which immediately splits open and sprays high into the air.

R. E.

One-at-a-Time Attack Rule. In any situation where the hero is alone, surrounded by dozens of bad guys, they will always obligingly attack one at a time. See any Schwarzenegger movie.

BARBARA KELSEY

One-Hour Hollywoodizing. No matter how wet or dirty they get, actors look good only one scene later. This is because movie stars have the Full-Body Scotchguard treatment done as soon as they hit it big. This works for casual water, sweat, drinks, blood, and all sorts of other fluids.

CHRISTOPHER G. JOHNSON

One Punch Fallacy. The myth that any movie hero can knock out any villain with a solid right to the jaw. (In any collision between a human skull and an unprotected human hand, the hand will be the worse for the experience.)

ANTHONY BRUCE GILPIN, *Riverside, Calif.*

One Sex at a Time. In any movie in which a man and a woman are both struggling with addiction, the protagonist man will find the strength to survive, but the woman will be destroyed. See *Clean and Sober, The Boost, Days of Wine and Roses,* etc.

FRAN PELZMAN LISCIO, *Upper Montclair, N.J.*

One-Trick Pony Rule

One Size Fits All (1). Any stolen clothing or shoes will perfectly fit any male character whether they were stolen from a clothesline or removed from a Nazi guard, police officer, lookout, etc., who was overpowered and whose identity the clothing thief has now assumed.

DONA KIGHT, *Chicago*

One Size Fits All (2). If a woman character steals clothing to disguise herself, the clothing, if male, will be too big. If female, it will be much too skimpy and revealing.

R. E.

One-Trick Pony Rule. Whenever a character displays an unusual talent or trick early in a thriller, it will later be used to save his or her life (e.g., Tom Cruise's gymnastics in *The Firm*).

MARTINA O'BOYLE, *Dallas*

Only One Man Can Rule. When it is stated that "only one man can (solve this crime, save the world, bring this man to justice, etc.)," you can be sure that that one man is now retired or was kicked off the force and must now be lured into action.

MERWYN GROTE, *St. Louis*

Oops, Sorry! Rule. Character sees person from behind on street, thinks it is someone he knows, runs up and confronts person, inevitably to discover it is someone else.

DAN SAUNDERS, *Oakland, Calif.*

Open Motel Bathroom Rule. In a low-budget action movie, when the hero is lying on the bed in a motel, watching TV, the door to the bathroom will be open, and the young female star will walk from the shower to the mirror in the bathroom, exposing her bare back, then turn to ask the hero a question.

DAVID STEVENS, *Irving, Tex.*

Orwell that Ends Wells. The inability of filmmakers to look into the future and see anything except cataclysmic wars, mass nuclear destruction, oppressive automation, uncontrollable crime, emotionally sterile environments, and ruthless police states in films like *1984, Sleeper, Back to the Future II, The Terminator, RoboCop, Brazil, Strange Days,* etc. Also see "Postapocalyptic Mechanical Darwinism."

MERWYN GROTE, *St. Louis*

Oscilloscope Fantastic. Test instruments are used to display Lissajous figures, sine waves, or other meaningless curves and lines to suggest that something mysteriously technical is happening in the laboratory.

CHARLES PEKLENK

Paint and Sufferink. Violent scenes in a G-rated animated feature which would have guaranteed the film at least a PG if it had been shot in live-action.

ANDY IHNATKO, *Westwood, Mass.*

Parent/Child Polarity Predictor. In the movies, if the parents are good the kids will be bad, or vice versa, unless they get along, in which case they're either both good or both bad.

STEVE WIDEMAN, *Birmingham, Ala.*

The above entry inspired the following exchange in the Answer Man column:

Q. You recently ran the following Movie Glossary entry: "In the movies, if the parents are good, the kids will be bad, or vice versa, unless they get along, in which case they're either both good or both bad." What other cases are there? CHRISTOPER G. JOHNSON, *Birmingham, Ala.* The Answer Man replied: "None. This splendid Glossary entry covers the entire range of possibilities."

R. E.

Parking Lot Shot. The long shot toward the end of the movie that causes a third of the audience to stand up, put on their coats, and head for the parking lot, whether or not the film is actually over.

ED SLOTA, *Providence, R.I.*

Party Movie. The gathering of a loose affiliation of stock players, friends, relatives, star wanna-bes, hangers-on, and professional acquaintances making cameo appearances under the vague notion that a movie is being made. At best, the host is Robert Altman and the end result is art *(Nashville, The Player)*. At worst, the host is Andy Warhol and the result is junk *(Lonesome Cowboys)*. Usually the host is like Burt Reynolds and the result is lowbrow entertainment (*Smoky and the Bandit, Hooper, The Best Little Whorehouse in Texas, Cannonball Run, Stroker Ace*). Woody Allen is king of the A-list Party Movies.

MERWYN GROTE, *St. Louis*

Pass Bypass Principle. Any theater that accepts passes will invariably exclude their use for any movie worth seeing.

MIKE SILVERMAN, *Holliston, Mass.*

Pathetic Fallacy, Demon Seed Division. There is a high correlation between thunderstorms and the births of children who will grow up to be evil. The storms grow more violent as the contractions get closer. When the child is born, the mother dies, thunder booms, and lightning reflects from the walls onto the face of the horrified midwife, who screams at the monstrous infant.

JERRY D. ROBERTS, *Hoover, Ala.*

Pavarotti Syndrome. When a superstar in one area tries to extend his success into movies by starring in a specially conceived vanity project. Examples: Luciano Pavarotti in *Yes, Giorgio*, Kurt Thomas in *Gymkata*, Mitch Gaylord in *American Anthem*, Evel Knievel in *Viva Knievel!*, Liberace in *Sincerely Yours*, Olivia Newton-John in *Xanadu*, Bruce Jenner and the Village People in *Can't Stop the Music*, Paul Simon in *One Trick Pony*, Bob Dylan in *Renaldo and Clara*, Neil Diamond in *The Jazz Singer*, Madonna's film career.

MERWYN GROTE, *St. Louis*

Peacenik Placard Rule. The person who paints the slogans must ensure that the peace sign is rendered without the vertical downward stroke. This ensures that the sign resembles the Mercedes-Benz logo as closely as possible.

MATTHEW COPE, *Montreal*

Pee Principle. Containers of urine in the movies have a surprisingly good change of being either spilled or drunk. See *Slums of Beverly Hills, Holy Man,* and *Dead Man on Campus.*

TOM MEYER, *Chicago*

Penguin Error. Bad guy keeps good guy alive to witness the great evil he will commit, allowing good guy to prevent it. See *Under Siege,* where the evil genius played by Tommy Lee Jones makes the fatal mistake of keeping Steven Seagal alive to witness the destruction of Honolulu. Named for the Penguin and all the other Batman enemies, who made this error weekly in the old series. See also "Fallacy of the Talking Killer."

JOSEPH HOLMES

Pentimento Paradigm. Pentimento is when images from an old painting seep through and become visible in a newer picture that has been painted over the old. The Pentimento Paradigm is when what we know about a filmmaker or actor seeps into our perception of his film work. Example: Any old Rock Hudson movie, now that his private life is no longer private. Being aware of the reality behind the fiction may add to the complexity of the drama (Taylor and Burton in *Who's Afraid of Virginia Woolf?*) or distract from its intentions (Woody and Mia in *Husbands and Wives*).

MERWYN GROTE, *St. Louis*

Perfectly Alternated Vehicle Rule. During all car chases through traffic, all of the vehicles not directly involved in the chase are arranged so that the chase vehicles can weave left and right continuously, as in a "Road and Track" handling test.

TOM RATCLIFFE, *Toronto*

Perk Girl. Used as an emblem of the hero's power. Appears in early scene, usually unclothed, with fashionable body. We usually do not see her face. She has no dialogue. She walks across the frame, a possession he takes for granted. Even though it seems from the context that they have an easy intimacy, we never see her again in the movie, nor is she ever referred to. See opening of *Wall Street*.

MICHAEL E. ISBELL

Perot Principle. The tendency of movie Texas billionaires to do the wackiest things. If they're not running for president, they're making loudmouthed fans the coach of their NBA team or willing a total stranger $10 million provided they find and marry any woman named Constantia Ruble by the end of the month.

ANDY IHNATKO, *Westwood, Mass.*

Personal Interest Rule. Any sequel using the advertising line, ". . . And this time, it's personal!" will have essentially the same plot as the first movie.

MARK MCDERMOTT, *Park Forest, Ill.*

Pet Homosexual. The lone gay man who establishes the characters' liberal tolerance as either the heroine's best friend (David Wayne in *Adam's Rib*, Roddy MacDowell in *Funny Lady*, James Coco in *Only When I Laugh*, George Carlin in *The Prince of Tides*, Rupert Everett in *My Best Friend's Wedding*, Nathan Lane in anything, etc.) or the sensitive extra person in a group (Greg Kinnear in *As Good as It Gets*, Steve Zahn in *Reality Bites*, Kris Kamm in *When the Party's Over*, Paul McCrane in *Fame*, Larry B. Scott in *Revenge of the Nerds*, etc.). He can talk incessantly about sex (Meshach Taylor in *Mannequin*), as long as he never actually has any.

MERWYN GROTE, *St. Louis*

Phantom Karaoke Machine. Unseen electronic prompter which explains how a small group of people who spontaneously take to a stage happen to know an entire number by heart, including harmonies and stage choreography. . . . Especially useful when the performers come from an era which precedes the song by decades.

ANDY IHNATKO, *Westwood, Mass.*

Phantom Phantom Rule. In any case where a movie crew member or unauthorized person accidentally appears in the background of a shot, a legend will develop to explain the appearance—usually involving suicide, a shotgun, and the spirit of the deceased haunting the set.

Phantom Karaoke Machine

Examples: the folklore surrounding *The Wizard of Oz* and *Three Men and a Baby*.

COLIN M. CHISHOLM

Phantom Photographer. A family's vacation snapshots always include every family member, even if they were twenty miles from the nearest neighbor. Who took the picture, the family dog?

ALESSANDRA KELLEY, *Chicago*

Phone Trace Game. When a criminal phones the police, he is kept talking as long as possible. However, since he always knows when to hang up, this process is never successful.

MAX THOMPSON, *Kent, England*

Physician, Heal Thyself. Any doctor taking on a tough case also has a problem of his own that the treatment of the patient will cure. Especially true of psychiatrists. See *Good Will Hunting*.

LEE FYOCK, *Natick, Mass.*

Pig Skin Movie. Any direct-to-video film about a female police officer going undercover in any sex-related industry (prostitute, stripper, phone-sex operator, etc.). Such movies usually feature Lorenzo Lamas or Leo Rossi in a costarring role.

DAWSON RAMBO, *Tucson, Ariz.*

Pillow Effect. When we see what is apparently a body under the covers of a bed, and the body is then fired at, the odds are good it's only carefully arranged pillows. This discovery often leads to a jailbreak, sneak attack, etc., by the person thought to be in the bed.

R. E.

Pill Rule. When a character is forced to take a pill, a later scene will show the character spitting the pill out.

JOHN GEKLE Jr., *Whiting, N.J.*

Ping Effect. When there is a movie close-up of a famous diamond, it inevitably emits a computer-generated sparkling flash, while there is a bright little "ping" on the sound track.

R. E.

Plot Pointer. Character who appears, delivers no more than a half-dozen lines of dialogue crucial to the plot, and then disappears for good. Plot Pointers are raised and trained exclusively for the movie industry on a free-range farm in Vermont, and descend from a breeding pair originally developed in 1932 for MGM musicals.

ANDY IHNATKO, *Westwood, Mass.*

Plugola Warning. If a movie trailer ends with a list of the artists on the film's sound track, there is an 80 percent chance the film will be terrible.

SCOTT HELD, *Dearborn, Mich.*

Plumber's Friend Rule. When a movie pans across a room while featuring the offscreen sound of energetic lovemaking, the actual source of the sound is invariably revealed as non–sex-related.

R. E.

Pocket Baffle. Handy liner that prevents a movie character's keys, coins, etc., from jingling until they are actually removed from his or her pocket. Never actually seen, but a theoretical necessity.

BRANNON MOORE, *Seattle*

Pointy Object Principle. If the bad guy attacks the good guy with a sharp object during a fight and it gets embedded in the wall or floor, the bad guy will be killed by it, generally by falling on it.

ERIC AMICK, *Columbia, Md.*

Poisoned Phone Booth. Any time the hero, on the run, stops at a phone booth to call for help, he inevitably reaches the person trying to kill him. The villain tells the hero to stay right there, then sends killers to finish him off. The hero wanders away and an unsuspecting extra enters the phone booth, where *he's* the one machine-gunned instead. Cut to: the hero, the horrified look on his face showing us he now understands The Full Extent of the Conspiracy.

DAVID DANIEL, *Smyrna, Ga.*

Police Escort Pause. Two police officers taking away an apprehended criminal will always pause as they pass the protagonist in order to allow the criminal to say something really nasty, vow revenge, or perhaps just spit.

JOSEPH HOLMES

Polite Killer Rule. It is a rule of horror etiquette that a monster must wait—all night if necessary—by a window in the intended victim's home until such time as he is effectively invited in by said victim opening a curtain and looking out of this window. Then and only then does the glass become breakable, and the monster or mad slasher is able to crash through and attack the intended target. This is an extension of the child's Monster under the Bed Rule (monsters under the bed cannot pull you off the bed unless you dangle a limb over the edge).

FRANK P. SCALFANO

Poor Phone Manners. No one ever says "good-bye" when talking on the phone in the movies. The conversation ends, according to the script, and the character just hangs up the phone.

DAWSON E. RAMBO, *Pelham Manor, N.Y.*

Pops Principle, The. In movies with teenage characters, there is usually a character named Pops who runs the local hangout or dance club.

DONALD MUNSCH, *Sherman, Tex.*

Portentous Porter Prognostication. In any movie featuring a mountain-climbing or jungle expedition employing native porters, the porters inevitably quit midway through the trek because of bad jou-jou, evil spirits, or some other seemingly silly portent of doom. The porters are inevitably proven to be right on the money.

Karl McBurnett, Euless, Tex.

PO Rule. No matter how many car chases, action set pieces, shoot-outs, or explosions have occurred, the villain is never really ready to be captured or killed until the hero picks himself up, dusts the broken glass off, sniffs the cordite in the air, and says, "Now he's really beginning to piss me off!"

Dawson E. Rambo, Pelham Manor, N.Y.

Possessed Golf Cart. Any layperson who gets behind the wheel of a golf cart will eventually drive the vehicle into the nearest body of water. (Cf. *Legal Eagles, Stakeout,* etc.)

Dan Gutowsky, Lansing, Mich.

Possible Implausible Rule. Movie audiences are quicker to accept the impossible than the implausible.

David Burd, East Stroudsburg, Pa.

Postapocalyptic Mechanical Darwinism. Doctrine that holds that in any movie set in the postapocalyptic future only the most destructive products of society will survive, i.e., guns, explosives, fast cars, nuclear devices, cigarettes. Common, plentiful, and beneficial things (toasters, telephones, indoor plumbing) will have perished from Earth. Example: In *Waterworld,* clumsy, impractical jet skis survived while millions of other boats, from dinghies to ocean liners, apparently did not.

Merwyn Grote, St. Louis

Preemptive Nudity Ratio. The probability of the female star being seen nude decreases in inverse proportion to the number of other nude women in the movie. See "Female Star in a Topless Bar Rule."

DAVID STEVENS, *Irving, Tex.*

Premature Disarmament (1). Movie heroes have a habit of optimistically tossing away their weapons too soon. This act is usually preceded by the Instant Diagnosis Syndrome, where the hero, after a first strike/punch/hit, wrongly decides after a cursory glance that the bad guy is unconscious, dead, or disabled.

HARRISON CHEUNG

Premature Disarmament (2). In horror films, after the monster has apparently been killed, the heroine inevitably drops her weapon, usually flinging it away in disgust. The monster is, of course, still alive.

R. E.

Prematurely Lightened Loads (aka, the "Leave It, It's Too Heavy and Besides it Might Save My Life" Syndrome). Situations where the good guy disables the first of many bad guys and when given the choice to take the bad guy's guns and ammo, doesn't do so. Also applies to water, radios, flare guns, car keys, maps, and the like.

ERIC M. DAVITT, *Toronto*

Premature Tune Out Rule. Guilty characters listening to reports of their escape always angrily switch off the news in midreport instead of listening for valuable information.

TOM KUENNEN, *Lincolnshire, Ill.*

Pre-1980 Matutinal Nonnudity Rule. Even if they have had four hours of rumpy-pumpy the previous night, when people get out of bed the next morning they always prudishly cover their exits with a sheet.

HILARY POTTS, *West Ealing, London*

Principle of Evil Marksmanship. The bad guys are always lousy shots in the movies. Three villains with Uzis will go after the hero, spraying thousands of rounds which miss him, after which he picks them off with a handgun.

JIM MURPHY, *New York City*

Principle of Inverse Critical Plausibility. The proven inverse relationship between the quality of a film and the number of rave reviews in its ads which originated from publications and TV shows with the word "Hollywood" in their titles.

ANDY IHNATKO, *Westwood, Mass.*

Principle of Pedestrian Pathology. Whenever a character on foot is being pursued by one in a car, the pedestrian inevitably makes the mistake of running down the middle of the street, instead of ducking down a narrow alley, into a building, behind a telephone pole, etc. All that saves such pedestrians is the fact that in such scenes the character on foot can always outrun the car.

STUART CLELAND, *Chicago*

Principle of Selective Lethality. The lethality of a weapon varies, depending on the situation. A single arrow will drop a stampeding bison in its tracks, but it takes five or six to kill an important character. A single bullet will always kill an extra on the spot, but it takes dozens to bring down the hero.

BARRY ZIMMERMAN

Product Displacement. The opposite of product placement: Peculiar practice in old movies and TV shows of disguising the brand names of products. A cereal box on the breakfast table might have a brightly colored rooster and the words "Corn Flakes" on it, but the word "Kellogg's" is absent, painted over so that the top third of the box is mysteriously blank. A police radio might announce an APB on a "1963 four-door gray sedan," but leave out the important fact that it is a Ford Fairlane.

MERWYN GROTE, St. Louis

Projection Rejection. Any scene taking place in a movie theater projection booth will feature old-fashioned, nostalgic reel-to-reel projectors, even though they have been out of date for at least two decades. No movie has ever shown modern automated platters. The projectionist will be a slow-moving old-timer, rather than an underpaid teenager.

MERWYN GROTE, St. Louis

Prop Recycling. Sci-fi/fantasy movies sometimes borrow futuristic devices from each other because of low budgets. Example: The ghost detectors in *Ghostbusters II* became motion detectors in *They Live*.

TERRY FOX

Proxy Plastic Surgery Rule. When a female star *uses* a body double for her nude scenes, the double will always have larger, firmer breasts.

DAVID STEVENS, Irving, Tex.

Psychic Flip. Amazing ability of any actor or actress to open a book to within five pages of the one they are looking for. If the proper page is not found on the first try, it will take no more than three flips to find it.

KYLE SIPPLES

Psychic Geographical Position Finder. When characters in a movie invite people they have just met over to their houses, they almost never give them their addresses, so they must have some sort of inner sensors that collect this information for them.

AMY CASH, Elmont, N.Y.

Psychic Partner. In countless cop movies: (1) Hero comes in the door of his apartment/house to a ringing phone. (2) Answering it, he hears his partner say something like, "You'd better turn on channel 3 *right now!* (3) The hero does so, only to see a news report *just beginning* that brings a crucial development or clue to the plot. Since the news report is just beginning, how did the partner know about it?

DAWSON E. RAMBO, Pelham Manor, N.Y.

Pull Over Rule. Whenever a cop pulls someone over in movie, he's nearly as certain to be killed as if he had just announced the number of days until his retirement.

IAN MANTGANI, Liverpool, England

Punkwear Syndrome. In any movie in which a gang of toughs suddenly jumps or in some way menaces the hero, one of them will always be wearing a tight knit shirt with horizontal black and white stripes, and a black vest.

FRAN PELZMAN LISCIO, Upper Montclair, N.J.

Push! Push! Scene. Obligatory natural childbirth scene, which is to boomer movies what the chase is in a Dirty Harry picture. Modern version of the old "boil water, hot water, and lots of it!" scene.

R. E.

QT Kiss of Death. If a hot new director is called "The next Quentin Tarantino," his next release will sink. This is very much akin to a singer being proclaimed "The next Dylan," or the *Sports Illustrated* cover jinx. Also applies to Tarantino.

MARK MCDERMOTT, Park Forest, Ill.

Quick Recovery Syndrome. Any person critical to the movie's sequel (such as the hero's buddy) can be on the edge of death throughout the film, but by the end of the movie recovers fully. See *Beverly Hills Cop II,* where Ronny Cox is shot in the heart at point-blank range but is ready to leave the hospital within seventy-two hours, or *Licence to Kill,* where Bond's newlywed buddy loses the lower half of his body to a shark, but is joking at the film's end.

TED MILLER, Green Bay, Wis.

Radar Bullet Phenomenon. A mysterious force which ensures that if a bullet does not hit a major character in an instantly lethal place (i.e., the head or heart), it won't hit any bones or vital organs, and will rarely do serious damage. In the truck chase in *Raiders of the Lost Ark,* for example, Indy is shot in the upper arm, from the side. The bullet doesn't break his arm, though from that angle it should, and he retains full use of his arm. Near the end of *RoboCop,* the bad guy shoots Murphy's partner Lewis half a dozen times with a large-caliber pistol, but she's still able to crawl twenty or thirty feet, and then lift, aim, and fire a huge rifle.

JON WOOLF, *Beavercreek, Ohio*

Radio Pictures. A character's dialogue describes what we can clearly see happening on the screen. Critic Rich Elias tags an all-time classic when he observes that Jack, in *Titanic,* says, "Let's get out of here! This place is flooded!"

TOM NORRIS, *Braintree, Mass.*

Rain as Emotion Syndrome. When an actor is unable to register shock, the director calls for rain and instructs the actor to make no attempt to avoid getting wet.

NIGEL SEARLE, *Venice, Fla.*

Rattlesnake Rectal Regulation. In any comedy set in the Old West, if a character lowers his pants to move his bowels, he will be horrified to find he has chosen a secluded spot that is home to a rattlesnake. See *City Slickers II* and *Lightning Jack.*

R. E.

Real Cut-Up. Medical examiners in the movies take great pleasure in displaying gallows humor when civilians (usually cops) come to visit. They're usually snacking or making very graphic comments in an effort to make the visitor sick. Examples: Gregory Hines in *Wolfen,* John Sayles in *The Howling,* M. Emmet Walsh in *White Sands,* Clint Howard in *Backdraft,* and one of the funniest examples, *The Enforcer.*

LEE STONEMAN, *El Reno, Okla.*

Rebellious Teenage Daughters. The teenage daughters of police officers/federal agents/private investigators always dress up like little tramps until the end of the movie, where they will reemerge as wholesome-girl-next-door types. See *The Last Boy Scout, True Lies, Face/Off.*

CHRISTOPHER M. TERRY, *Atlanta, Ga.*

Relevant Telephone Syndrome. In police headquarters, all calls are directly relevant to the case at hand. There is never a scene where the phone rings and the detective speaks, hangs up, and says, "That was *Better Homes and Gardens* magazine. They wanted to know if I wanted to renew my subscription."

RICK BENGE, *Vienna, Austria*

Remote Clicking Syndrome. Whenever anyone in a movie points a remote at the TV, the Foley artists always feel compelled to add clicks to the sound track so that we all know that they are changing channels. "Clicking" remotes disappeared around 1970.

MICHAEL G. MURASHKO, *Los Angeles*

Retreads. In many car chase scenes, skid marks already exist on the road before the car spins out, indicating either that the vehicle was moving so fast that its tires got there four seconds before the rest of the car, or that we're watching a third, fourth, or fifth take of the stunt.

ANDY IHNATKO, Westwood, Mass.

Reverse Discrimination. Whoever backs up in a horror movie is about to die.

DON HOWARD, San Jose, Calif.

Reverse Doppler Effect. Phenomenon only found in movies where an incoming artillery shell is heard decreasing in pitch. I was quite surprised in Vietnam when, during the course of a mortar attack, the shells were heard to increase in pitch, as any physics student could have predicted.

JOHN D. MCCLUSKEY

Reynolds Ramp. Heavy steel sewer pipes, railroad ties, or piles of dirt left in the road which cause cars to jump, flip, and/or barrel-roll in spectacular slow-motion fashion when they pass over them. N.B.: Force of attraction between a car and a Reynolds Ramp increases geometrically with the value, age, and scarcity of the car in question. No car driven by Burt Reynolds can avoid one.

ANDY IHNATKO, Westwood, Mass.

Rising Sidewalk. No female character in an action film can flee more than fifty feet before falling flat on her face. Someone then has to go back and help her up, while the monster/villain/enemy gains ground.

JAMES PORTANOVA, Fresh Meadows, N.Y.

Rock 'n' Roll Rule

Rock Candy Postulate. No hero is ever cut by glass while leaping through windows.

DANIEL ALVARADO, *Arleta, Calif.*

Rock 'n' Roll Lite Rule. Whenever a fictitious rock star sings or plays, the music will be wildly cheered by thousands of screaming fans, even though it isn't fit for a Kmart opening.

SAM WAAS, *Houston*

Rock 'n' Roll Rule. At a pivotal moment in an action movie when the hero is about to jet into space or attack the bad guys, he will shout, "Let's rock and roll!"

WILL GRIFFIN, *Bristol, England*

Rolling Stone Star Turn. A star accepts a big paycheck, doesn't like the movie he or she made, and publicly blames the director, writer, other actors, producer, agent, manager, etc. By dissociating self with picture, the actor hopes to reduce the number of viewers who will actually witness their halfhearted performance. Named for Sharon Stone's dissing of *Diabolique* prior to its release. Also see Sylvester Stallone re: *Judge Dredd* and Marlon Brando before *The Freshman.*

TOM COLGAN, *Algonquin, Ill.*

Roll Over, Beethoven. Any character seen intently enjoying classical music (especially opera) will do evil. Any character seen dancing and grooving to rock and roll will redeem and enlighten.

NEIL MILSTED, *Chicago*

Roto-Rooter Rule. The badness of a movie is directly proportional to the number of helicopters in it.

DAVE BARRY, *from* 25 Things I Have Learned in 50 Years

Rotten Teeth Display. Characters with really bad teeth spend most of their time with their mouths gaping open and their lips pulled back, as if to say "Hey–these teeth took three hours of makeup, so we might as well get our money's worth!"

R. E.

Rover, Dead Rover Rule. In any movie that begins with lowering skies and ominous music, all dogs being taken on walks in the countryside discover dead bodies.

R. E.

Rubbing It In. If a character has been injured earlier, the wound will be punched during the final fight, causing great but short-lived pain.

ANNA LAUX, *Ft. Wayne, Ind.*

Rube Goldberg Breakfast Device. Device that automatically makes breakfast as the hero is waking up. This appears early in films (usually children's films) to establish a wacky or eccentric inventor/scientist. For example: *Chitty Chitty Bang Bang.* In *Back to the Future,* it even fed the dog. Other examples: *Honey, I Shrunk the Kids* (only American one with an oatmeal maker); *Pee-wee's Big Adventure* (cracked an egg with toy bobbing bird; all flapjacks stayed on ceiling); *Casper* (established Casper's father, never seen, as inventor; had Personal Grooming Device); *The Wrong Trousers* (also had PGD, and foreshadowed technology gone wrong); *A Close Shave* (had semiautomatic porridge shooter); *Flubber* (ground the coffee beans in nice yuppie touch, cracked egg with laser).

BETSY LAWLOR and COLIN LAWLOR SANDERS, *Riverside, Calif.*

Rule of Chronic Tunnel Vision. In a horror movie, the character being stalked has vision limited to the camera's field of view. Therefore, anyone coming at any angle not directly ahead will invariably scare the living daylights out of him or her.

DANIEL ALVARADO, *Arleta, Calif.*

Rule of Concurrent Gestation. Any two women who are pregnant in the same movie will deliver at the same time. See *Father of the Bride II, Micki and Maude, Nine Months, Junior.*

DOUG THOMAS, *Seattle*

Rule of Detective's Girlfriend's ESP. Whenever another woman kisses a detective, his girlfriend picks this moment to walk in and see them. See *Who Framed Roger Rabbit, Dick Tracy.*

LUIS JACOBO, *Tulare, Calif.*

Rule of Reverse Explosive Proportionality. The quality of a movie containing an explosion is in roughly reverse proportion to the number of times that same explosion is

Rule of the Purloined Letter

shown from different angles. Example: The exploding van is shown four times in the movie *Dead Heat,* earning it a one-star rating.

MARTIN VASKO, San Francisco

Rule of the Hallucinogenic Carousel. Any time the hero or heroine is being pursued and the chase leads to a merry-go-round, the villain will be unable to catch his prey. Rather than wait ten seconds for the carousel to complete a revolution, the villain will immediately hop on in hot pursuit. During the chase the audience is often treated to weird calliope music. No real carousel uses such music; it sounds as if the sound track was switched with the fun house.

JOHN E. ROCHE, San Francisco

Rule of the Purloined Letter. When a character's mail has been regularly intercepted, all letters will be carefully preserved by the interceptor. There will be a heart-touching scene at the end where the character finally gets all of those letters and reads them one by one.

ANDY IHNATKO, Westwood, Mass.

Saliva Syndrome. Heroines who are tied up have an uncanny compulsion to spit in the villain's face. In response, the villain inevitably smiles.

R. E.

Sarandon-Mirren Rule. The best nude scenes are done by women who no longer have to do them for career reasons.

DAVID STEVENS, Irving, Tex.

Satin Static Cling Phenomenon. The heroine, after spending the night cavorting with a man she met only a few hours earlier, carefully pulls up the bedsheet to modestly cover herself when he says good-bye the next morning. Amazingly, the sheets stay in place even while she is sitting up. This rule does not apply in movies in which Madonna or Sharon Stone appear.

ALAN JOHNSON, *Phoenix*

Scary Old Man (or Woman). Used in horror movies to warn the young people to stay away from the old house, castle, woods, etc. Usually portrayed as a homeless person or someone that all the townspeople regard as crazy. See *Friday the 13th* movies.

EUGENE ACCARDO, *Brooklyn, N.Y.*

Sci-Fi Currency Conversion. In any science-fiction movie, anywhere in the galaxy, currency is refered to as "credits."

SAM HUMPHRIES

Screech in Time. When the protagonist in a movie needs to get across the street in a hurry, he or she inevitably comes within an eyelash of getting hit by the obligatory car which screeches to a halt only two inches away. Once this phenomena has occurred, the hero has no more problems getting to the other side.

RUSTY SOUTHWICK, *Orem, Utah*

Seagal Severity Scale. The closer together Steven Seagal's eyebrows are, the more violent the next scene.

DAWSON RAMBO, *Tucson, Ariz.*

Sean Connery Exception. Bald men are not allowed to perform romantic kissing in the movies unless they are later revealed to be villains, or are Sean Connery.

R. E.

Second Car Rule: Any fruit cart, plate-glass window, slow-moving camel, or other impediment not encountered by the first car in a chase must necessarily be encountered by the second one, usually to cheap comic effect. (First car narrowly misses two guys carrying plate-glass window. They breathe a sigh of relief. Then second car smashes it.)

TIM CARVELL, New York, N.Y.

Secretary Rule. In any scene where a character barges into someone else's office (boss, coworker, enemy), the bargee's secretary will always scold the character, warning him or her not to go into the office. The character will then disregard the warning and go in anyway, which leaves the secretary trying to stop the intrusion to no avail.

ROB WOLEJSZA, Astoria, N.Y.

Seeing-Eye Man. Function performed by most men in Hollywood feature films. Involves a series of shots in which (1) the man sees something, (2) he points it out to the woman, (3) she then sees it too, often nodding in agreement, gratitude, amusement, or relief.

First identified by LINDA WILLIAMS

Seeing Stars. In any space movie, stars must be visible in the background of all exterior space shots—even though, in reality, there is no camera or film sensitive enough to pick them up without overexposing whatever is in the foreground.

GERALD FITZGERALD, *Dallas*

"See You Next Wednesday." This line was used in the telephone call from space in Stanley Kubrick's *2001,* and has since been used in every single film directed by John Landis. For that matter, Kubrick had a scene involving a bathroom in every one of *his* films.

R. E.

Self-Help Lane. When movie heroes crash a high-society party, they head straight for a beautiful lady, and are always able to trap two drinks from the tray of a passing waiter before reaching their lovely destination.

ALEXIS S. MENDEZ, *Aguadilla, Puerto Rico*

Self-Orchestrating Piano. When the musician hero starts dreaming up a piano concerto, the piano can somehow summon up a full orchestra to accompany itself within twenty-five seconds. Some singers can also do this.

HILARY POTTS, *West Ealing, London*

Semi-Obligatory Lyrical Interlude (Semi-OLI). Scene in which soft focus and slow motion are used while a would-be hit song is performed on the sound track and the lovers run through a pastoral setting. Common from the mid-1960s to the mid-1970s; replaced in 1980s with the Semi-Obligatory Music Video (q.v.).

R. E.

Semi-Obligatory Music Video (Semi-OMV). Three-minute sequence within otherwise ordinary narrative structure, in which a song is played at top volume while movie characters experience spasms of hyperkinetic behavior and stick their faces into the camera lens. If a band is seen, the Semi-OMV is inevitably distinguished by the director's inability to find a fresh cinematic approach to the challenge of filming a slack-jawed drummer.

R. E.

Send in the Clones. If a computer is used early in a film, every subsequent computer will have exactly the same operating system, display typeface, and command structure, and will conform to any special hardware or software modifications or enhancements made to any computer prior to that point in the movie.

BRANNON MOORE, *Seattle*

Sequel. A filmed deal.

R. E.

Seven Minute Rule. In the age of the seven-minute attention span (inspired by the average length between TV commercials), action movies aimed at teenagers are constructed out of several seven-minute segments. At the

Shelley Winters Index

end of each segment, another teenager is dead. When all the teenagers are dead (or, if you arrived in the middle, when the same dead teenager turns up twice), the movie is over.

R. E.

Sex-Specific Disintegrating Outfit. When the male and female characters in a trashy action movie go to hell and back, only the woman's clothing begins to disintegrate.

DAVE POLSKY, *Ottawa, Canada*

Sex-Specific Sticky Sheet Technique. The large seam at the top edge of sheets used in movies is covered with a sex-specific adhesive, causing the sheet to stick firmly to the upper breast area of women, while inches away, the same sheet clings above the man's waist.

DAVID STEVENS, *Irving, Tex.*

Shelley Winters Index. In scenes where a character must hold his or her breath and swim underwater, the elapsed time in seconds between the "pfoooahh!" of the last audience member giving up trying to match the time, and the character's finally reaching a supply of air. For instance, in *The Abyss,* Ed Harris's SWI is 3.2; in *Star Trek IV* William Shatner's is 40.0; and in *The Poseidon Adventure* Shelley Winters herself racks up an impressive SWI of 149.9.

ANDY IHNATKO, *Westwood, Mass.*

Shoe of Threat. When a POV shot shows a victim crawling toward the camera on the floor, chances are he will eventually come upon a shoe. As he looks up, the camera will tilt to show a menacing figure towering above him.

R. E.

Short Life Syndrome. Night watchmen in horror movies have a life expectancy of twelve seconds.

SAM WAAS, *Houston*

Short Time Syndrome. Applies to prison, war, or police movies, where the hero only has a few more days until he is free, his tour is over, or he can retire with full pension. Whenever such a character makes the mistake of mentioning his remaining time ("Three days and I'm outta here!") he will die before the end of that time.

R. E.

Silent Death Rule. Whenever movie characters are shot with a gun with a silencer, they cooperate by dying quietly.

NATE MARMUR, *Rochester, N.Y.*

Simultaneous Recovery Syndrome. When a group of movie characters is rendered unconscious, all characters awake at approximately the same time.

JEFF BRAUN, *Seattle,* and BILL RUSSELL, *Richmond, Ind.*

Sinatra's Law. In any Odd Couple Formula movie, the buddies will run into a situation in which the normal partner is unable to function successfully. The other partner, representing the eccentric, abnormal, and supposedly wrong way of doing things, will invariably say, "Let's try doing it . . . my way." (E.g., Eddie Murphy in *48 HRS,* Mel Gibson in *Lethal Weapon,* etc.)

PATRICK DORSEY, *Huntington, N.Y.*

Single Bullet Rule: Whenever two characters are struggling for a gun, it must discharge one (1) bullet before the struggle is resolved. No more, no less.

TIM CARVELL, *New York, N.Y.*

Sinister Stretch Limo Rule. Movie villains are often chauffeured in black stretch limos with darkly tinted windows. This does not make them an object of curiosity in the rundown warehouse districts or dangerous inner city streets where they usually are found. See also "Limo Exclusion Law."

R. E.

Siskel's Test. "Is this film more interesting than a documentary of the same actors having lunch?"

GENE SISKEL

Siskel's Theory of Relativity. The movie is moving slowly when you begin to look at your watch. It is moving very slowly when you begin to tap your watch to be sure it hasn't stopped.

GENE SISKEL

Skoal Rule. Any non–sports-related character who chews tobacco is evil. All sports-related characters who chew tobacco are good.

DAWSON RAMBO, Tucson, Ariz.

Slap of Commitment. Moment in any film when the hero and heroine argue heatedly about how much they hate one another, escalating to the point when the heroine slaps the hero–followed by their passionate embrace.

PATRICK RODUIN, Seattle

Slide Show Rule. During briefings about the search for a sinister international criminal, the chief good guy will hold a magic lantern show, projecting a blurry picture of the bad guy and intoning, "He's a former member of the KGB/IRA/Red Brigade." (Cf. *Nighthawks, In the Line of Fire.*)

CHRIS FISANICK, Barnesboro, Pa.

SloMo Team Saunter. Depending on when in the movie this occurs, this sequence has two meanings. At the beginning of the movie, over the title credits, the SloMo Team Saunter is designed for us to see "The Team" as a single unit, so that later, we know who the Good Guys are. In an action/adventure movie, the SloMo Team Saunter will let us know that training has finished, and that some serious butt-kicking is about to commence. In sports, especially kid-based sports movies, the SMTS is designed to let us know that the disparate collection of misfits has come together as one, and also, serious butt-kicking is about to commence. Any movie made after *Reservoir Dogs,* with saunter will resemble the gait and placement of the characters in that movie.

DAWSON RAMBO, *Tucson, Ariz.*

Smoothly Gliding Death. Any time the movie leaves a scene by cutting to a slow tracking shot looking at the back of a supporting character sitting at a desk or table while working hard on some task or project critical to the good guys' victory, that character is about to die.

BRANNON MOORE, *Seattle*

Snicker-Snack Effect. In horror movies, whenever we see a knife with a big, shiny blade, we inevitably hear the scrape of metal against metal, even if it touches nothing.

R. E.

Snoozers' Synopsis. For the convenience of audience members who slept through part of a film, there is usually a loud noise in association with the climax, followed by a speech in which the hero explains what the movie was all about. See *Stripes* (Murray to the troops), *The 'Burbs* (Hanks on his lawn), *Purple Rose of Cairo* (Tom's movie "self" before he reenters the movie screen). Especially true of stories that end in a courtroom or similar setting: *Quiz Show* (the hearing), *Ghosts of Mississippi* (the trial), *Scent of a Woman* (the hearing).

PAUL WIEDER, Chicago

Snore-Snort Syndrome. When the hero absolutely, positively, has to stay awake during a critical stakeout he'll inevitably fall asleep. But his nodding head will jolt him back awake at just the right moment, five seconds before the crisis.

CHRIS TROISE, New York, N.Y.

Sorceresses' Cackle. All movie characters who play witches, voodoo priestesses, black magic practitioners, etc., end enigmatic statements with an evil cackle.

R. E.

Sound Track Cautionary Rule. Don't bother with any movie where the ads devote more attention to the performers whose music is on the sound track than to the plot or the actors.

STEVEN STIEN, Buffalo Grove, Ill.

Sound Track Surprise. Occurs when the audience members think the song they are hearing is just part of the sound track and not being heard by the characters, but it suddenly ends when a character turns off the stereo or radio.

KYLE L. CAIN, Sugar Land, Tex.

Space Alien Rule. No matter how strange a space alien looks or how far away he comes from, he will always be a binaural, bipedal humanoid with two arms.

GERALD FITZGERALD, Dallas

Spacious Poverty Rule. "Cramped quarters" in a film (cramped big-city studio apartments, college dorm rooms, hospital and motel rooms) are invariably much more spacious than any available in real life.

KRIS CORRADETTI, Youngstown, Ohio

Sparks and Steam Factory. In action movies, the chase inevitably leads to the interior of a factory where showers of sparks fall to the floor, and great clouds of steam billow up from below. As nearly as the audience can determine, these are the factory's only products.

R. E.

Spinning Image Flipover. The use of an optical printer to spin the picture to create the unconvincing illusion that a car is rolling over in a car accident.

MERWYN GROTE, St. Louis

Split the Difference Ending. Movies about exaggeratedly masculine main characters caught in a moral dilemma in which there's no clear-cut "right" answer usually end by splitting the difference so that the hero can be right and wrong at the same time. This satisfies the emotional needs of the audience at the expense of logic, realism, or morality. See *White Squall, Crimson Tide.*

RICH ELIAS, Delaware, Ohio

Stab the Priest and Shoot the Blind Man Syndrome.
When moviemakers are afraid their villain is becoming
too sympathetic, they have him perform a dastardly act
immediately before he is killed. That is the only reason
Kirk Douglas stabs a priest in *The Vikings* and Gene
Hackman shoots a blind man in *The Quick and the Dead.*
                                    WAYNE KLATT, *Chicago*

Stalled Truck Technique. Whenever a cop is chasing
quarry in an alley, a truck will back into the alley, cutting
off the cop. The truck then mysteriously becomes rooted
to the spot, and the cop jumps out of the car. Cut to: the
quarry getting away. Cut back to: the cop pounding the
roof of his car. (In rural movies, substitute narrow dirt
road for alley, and farm tractor for truck.) See also "Camel,
Slow-Moving."
                        MICHAEL J. PILLING, *Maple Ridge, B.C., Canada*

Stanton-Walsh Rule. No movie featuring either Harry
Dean Stanton or M. Emmet Walsh in a supporting role
can be altogether bad. Exceptions are *Chattahoochee,*
starring Walsh, and *Wild at Heart,* starring Stanton.

                                                        R. E.

Stardom Uncertainty Principle. The introduction of a
major star into a perfect screenplay will diminish it in
unpredictable ways.

                                                        R. E.

Stealth Helicopters. Although the helicopter is one of
the loudest machines in existence, movie characters never

hear a helicopter until they actually see it appearing in the window, rising over a bridge, etc.

SHARI C. PARKER, *Chicago*

Stepford Babe. In any movie in which the protagonist is a moron who farts, curses, swears, stumbles, trips over things, and grows warts on his forehead, the serene Babe he falls for never notices how repulsive and idiotic he constantly appears, except to occasionally evince mild surprise. See *Happy Gilmore, Beverly Hills Ninja, The Nutty Professor, High School High, Ace Ventura, The Waterboy,* etc.

FRAN PELZMAN LISCIO, *Upper Montclair, N.J.*

Still Out There Somewhere. Obligatory phrase in Dead Teenager and Mad Slasher Movies, where it is triggered by the words, "The body was never found. They say he/she is . . ."

R. E.

Stinking Badges Drawer. Special drawer in the desk of every police chief where he keeps the badges of cops he's put on suspension. Usually has only one badge in it, though, because he can always reach into it and, without looking, grab the badge of the cop who is the hero of the movie.

BRIAN JONES

Stompworthies. Interchangeable movie extras, usually appearing in ethnically mixed groupings of three or more, whose job is to act unruly and obnoxious in a public place, thus necessitating a photogenic pummeling (invariably topped with a zippy one-liner) by the film's action-hero.

JEFF LEVIN, *Rochester, N.Y.*

Stradivarius Rule. Whenever a violin is an important part of a movie plot, it is a Stradivarius. Whenever such an instrument does appear on the screen, it is, of course, doomed.

BOB GOODMAN, *New York University*

"Stranger in a Strange Land" Principle. When a star of a movie shows up in a new town, that person will be famous in that town by the end of the movie.

R. E.

Streep Throat. Malady affecting vocal chords of movie characters. Symptoms commence at the point at which an actor decides that keeping up a difficult Brooklyn (or South Boston, Irish, Hungarian, etc.) accent is more trouble than it is worth.

ANDY IHNATKO, *Westwood, Mass.*

Street Furniture Rules. (1) All movies set prior to 1955 should have yellow and black stop signs. (2) All movies set prior to 1982 should lack *USA Today* boxes.

HANK OTTERY, *Chicago*

Stupid Adult Rule. In any situation where a child or teenager finds that the group is in danger, or has the solution to a problem that stumps all the adults, the adults will invariably refuse to listen to the kid. This continues

Stradivarius Rule

either until it's almost too late, or until the kid takes matters into his or her own hands. Especially likely in any episode of "Star Trek" where Wesley Crusher appears.

ANDREW COLES, *Toronto*

Sturgeon's Law. "Ninety percent of everything is crap." (First formulated in the 1950s by the science-fiction author Theodore Sturgeon; quoted here because it so manifestly applies to motion pictures.)

Substandard Movie Tires. Movie characters have worn tires on their cars. Even an easy stop from five miles an hour produces a skidding sound as if the brakes were locked from thirty miles an hour. Comfortably rounding a corner causes tire squealing. Even the wimpiest of cars makes a brief burning-rubber sound as it gently accelerates from a stop.

JIM COLLIER, *Dallas*

Superfluous Loudspeaker Rule. Automated announcements in movies exist only for atmosphere, and say useless things: "This is the third floor. This is the third floor."

HANNO MUELLER, *Hamburg, Germany*

Superfluous Pump. Dramatic effect in gun movies. The gunman has fired multiple shots and then when he has his victim cornered, unnecessarily pumps (cocks) his weapon, an action that would eject an unused shell.

J. FERGUSON, *Elmhurst, Ill.*

Supporting Sweat. Whenever a main character is in a steam room, a supporting character will have to enter the steam room while still wearing a suit and a tie. This will lead to the usual sweating, fidgeting, loosening of the tie, etc.

FRANK MOUTON, *Sacramento, Calif.*

Surprise Gender Switch. In any competition where one of the opponents is wearing a garment that conceals body and face, if that opponent wins, in the next shot the head-covering is pulled off to reveal—gasp!—that the opponent was a woman!

R. E.

Surround Sound Reciprocal Principle. The amount of surround sound track usage is inversely proportional to the amount of dialogue worth hearing.

DAVID KALIN, *San Francisco*

SWAT Movie. Sinks Without a Trace.

RICH ELIAS, *Delaware, Ohio*

Technopyromania. Affliction that compels filmmakers and special effects people to depict the malfunction of computers as being accompanied by smoke, flames, showers of pyrotechnic sparks, frenzied flashing lights, and wildly spinning tape drives spewing tape into the air.

PAUL A. LEE, *Germantown, Wis.*

Teeny-Prole. An actor who looks like a handsome teenage model, playing a character who is allegedly a hardened proletarian (e.g., Johnny Depp in *Donnie Brasco,* Keanu Reeves in *Speed,* etc.).

R. E.

Teetotaler Relapse Syndrome. Any character introduced as a recovering alcoholic who's been off the bottle for an extended period will go back to drinking sometime during the film. Examples: Michael Douglas in *Basic Instinct,* Kenneth Branagh in *Peter's Friends,* Claire Danes in *The Mod Squad.*

JEFF LEVIN, Rochester, N.Y.

"Tell Me Where You Are and I'll Come and Get You." Telltale line that finally makes obvious to everyone (except the hero) that the hero's trusted friend or supervisor has gone over to the bad guys.

JIM LEE, Cary, N.C.

Telltale File Giveaway. Any time the good guy surreptitiously pilfers from a file cabinet, something will happen to force him to flee the scene shortly after discovering the needed secret information. His hasty departure will cause him to leave the file in a state that allows the bad guy to deduce who was there.

RICK NEWBY, College Place, Wash.

Ten Kickboxing Movies Still to Be Made: (1) *A Kickboxer Christmas;* (2) *Kalifornia Kickboxer;* (3) *Where the Kickboxers Are;* (4) *Kickboxing in Fruit;* (5) *Kickboxer Karwash;* (6) *Oh to be Kickboxing;* (7) *Nick: The Kickboxer*

Teeny-Prole

Who Couldn't Read; (8) *So Many Kickboxers;* (9) *Jaws VII: The Kickboxer;* (10) *Kickboxer VI, Jaws II.*

ADAM PLANTINGA, *Grand Rapids, Mich.,*
and HADLEY BETH, *Urbana, Ill.*

Thanks, but No Thanks. When two people have just had a heart-to-heart conversation, as Person A starts to leave room, Person B says (tentatively) "Bob?" A pauses, turns, and says "Yes?" B says, "Thanks."

BETSEY BRUNK

Thanks for Nothing! Of all the holidays on the calendar, Thanksgiving is the one most often chosen by the movies to show dysfunctional families in meltdown. The title card "Thanksgiving," indeed, is almost a guarantee that shameful secrets, towering rages, and massive depression will be presented, along with a vast amount of alcohol abuse. See *Home for the Holidays, The Ice Storm, The House of Yes, Unhook the Stars, The Myth of Fingerprints.*

R. E.

Theological Revisionism, Angel Division. Movies seem unaware that all world religions teach that angels are disembodied spirits without gender. They consistently confuse angels with reincarnated souls and with ghosts, leading to the problem of angels who take physical form, fall in love, eat hot dogs, decide to become human, etc. All of these actions are against the angel rules. See *The Preacher's Wife, City of Angels,* etc.

R. E.

Theory of Movie Relativity. If you watch the credits to the very end you will see at least one person listed who has the same last name as the director or one of the producers.

DAVID BURD, East Stroudsburg, Pa.

Therapeutic Child Law. If a character is introduced as hating children, he or she will like them by the end, and probably will have saved one from a life-threatening situation somewhere along the line.

TOM CAMMALLERI, Santa Barbara, Calif.

There-Goes-the-Neighborhood Rule. In horror movies, no matter how many ghostly apparitions or psychokillers appear in a house, the owners will not leave it. In fact, the more scared they get, the more determined they are to stay put. Apparently they're earning some kind of "scream equity." See *Amityville Horror,* etc.

RAPHAEL CARTER, Tempe, Ariz.

Third Hand. Invisible appendage used by Rambo in *Rambo,* in the scene where he hides from the enemy by completely plastering himself inside a mud bank. Since it is impossible to cover yourself with mud without at least one hand free to do the job, Rambo must have had a third, invisible hand. This explains a lot about the movie.

R. E.

Thirty-Minute Nudity Rule. If there is no female nudity in the first thirty minutes of a movie, there won't be any later. This rule is inviolable in made-for-cable movies.

DAVID STEVENS, Irving, Tex.

Three-Bill, No Change, Five-Second Rule. In movies, when paying for an item in a store, the customer always pays the clerk with no more than three bills. The clerk never offers change, even if the charge is $17.63. The whole transaction takes no more than five seconds.

Clay Waldrop Jr., *Garland, Tex.*

Three Little Words. When someone says, "I've never seen him before in my life," those last three words guarantee it's a lie.

Greg Brown, *Chicago, Ill.*

Three-Minute Mark. No matter how empty a theater is, someone will take the seat directly in front of you within three minutes after the lights are dimmed, thus partially obstructing your previously clear view of the screen.

Merwyn Grote, *St. Louis*

Three's a Crowd Rule. In any movie where the protagonist, his sidekick, and another character are all working to solve a mystery, the third person will usually betray the other two (or will have been working against them all along). See Tom Sizemore's character in *Strange Days,* the taxi driver in *Total Recall,* many others.

Gregor Gilliom, *Columbus, Ohio*

Throw 'em Back Syndrome. Whenever characters in a movie catch a fish they have been after for at least fifteen years, they always let it go because it has been a worthy opponent. Of course nobody believes them when they say they caught him. See *Grumpier Old Men, On Golden Pond,* etc.

Jon Pietrowski, *Genoa, Ohio*

193

Throw 'em Back Syndrome

Tic Reversi. Nervous disorder that causes an actor to repeatedly pick up and put down an item upon each cut between reverse shots in a scene.

PAUL A. LEE, Germantown, Wis.

Tijuana. In modern Horny Teenager Movies, performs the same symbolic function as California did for the beatniks, Marakech did for the hippies, and Paris did for the Lost Generation.

R. E.

Timely Bladder Syndrome. When hero is one of a group of people, he goes off to the toilet or other secluded room just as the villains attack. Glimpsing the action from the bathroom, he is unknown to the bad guys and thus still free to respond. See *Die Hard* (back room), *Under Siege* (meat locker), *Passenger 57* (airplane toilet).

KEVIN WAN, Seattle

Time Waits for No Director. The minute hand on a clock always clicks the moment the camera cuts to it.

R. E.

Title Tease Warning. Movies that alternate long passages of plot with opening credits for lengthy periods of screen time reflect the attention span of their creators and should be avoided.

R. R. KUNZ

Traction Action Rule

Tonight Show Validation. Public humiliation is always represented in the movies by Jay Leno's jokes.

IAN MANTGANI, *Liverpool, England*

Too-Soon Apology. Whenever one character seems to have died, and his best friend arrives just seconds too late to have saved him, the best friend must stand over his buddy's body and confess to wronging his dead friend in some way ("Remember when Bettylou stood you up for the prom? Well, she was actually sneaking off to see me!"). The dead friend will inevitably turn out to have been merely wounded. Wacky hijinks ensue.

TIM CARVELL, *New York, N.Y.*

Traction Action Rule. Whenever there's a patient in traction with a cast on his leg and ropes attached to a pulley system, a visitor will inevitably cause the cast to go up into the air and the patient to experience severe pain.

RAUL H. MARQUEZ, Maryland

Training Sequence. In any movie culminating in a competition, this is the montage during which the hero is turned from a loser into a winner through the inspired but merciless tutelage of the Coach Figure, who alternates between wisdom and sadism. See Pat Morita in *The Karate Kid*, Burgess Meredith in *Rocky*, John Candy in *Cool Runnings*, etc. The training inevitably includes one lesson that will be remembered in a flashback during a crucial moment of the competition, giving the hero fresh inspiration.

R. E.

Treasure Map Thunderstorm Rule. In any film involving a treasure hunt, the characters find the map in an old dusty attic while it is raining outside. The characters stand with their backs to a window, looking at the map. When they realize its importance, there is always a thunderous boom and a bolt of lightning in the window. See *The Goonies* and *City Slickers II*.

JEANNE KENNELLY, Chicago

TRISHA Phenomenon. The ability of the technical names of all movie computers to improbably collapse into a cute acronym, usually a female name (e.g., "Triply-Recursive Iteratively Symbolic Hierarchical Analyzer").

ANDY IHNATKO, Westwood, Mass.

Tucco's Advice. Named for the character played by Eli Wallach in *The Good, the Bad and the Ugly*. It comes in the scene where Tucco is taking a bath, and a guy bursts in the room, promising Tucco he will have vengeance on him. At that moment, Tucco kills him. Tucco then advises the corpse, "If you have to shoot, shoot! Don't talk." See also "Fallacy of the Talking Killer."

STEPHEN J. BAUGHMAN

Turning a Deaf Ear. Movie heroes squeeze off hundreds of rounds of ammo but suffer no hearing loss. For example, in *Rambo III*, Rambo enters a metal warehouse and runs an entire belt of ammo through his M-60 machine gun. Afterward he carries on a whispered conversation with the evil CIA man in another room.

JOSEPH HOLMES

Turn It Off Rule. Immediately after the radio or TV reports something important to the plot, someone must always reach over and turn it off.

KYLE L. CAIN, *Sugar Land, Tex.*

Turtle Effect. Once characters are knocked down, they just lie there as if unable to get up (e.g., Sigourney Weaver in *Alien*).

JAMES PORTANOVA, *Fresh Meadows, N.Y.*

Two-Faced Blouse. In movie scenes where an actress is auditioning for a director, one of the standard demands is that she take off her blouse and expose her breasts. Typically, the actress does not want to do this because she feels it violates her as a person. There are two possible outcomes: (1) she refuses, and stalks out; (2) she agrees, and bares her breasts. If the choice is (2), it's interesting how many filmmakers allow the audience to see her breasts, instead of choosing a different angle. That means the filmmaker is going along with the humiliation, and expects us to enjoy it too.

R. E.

Two-Hat Trick. Hero wears cool hat, sidekick wears goofy hat.

R. E.

Two Sentence Rule. Any character who is introduced more than halfway through an action movie and (a) has a dialogue of more than two sentences with a major character, or (b) reveals to a major character that he or she has reached a milestone (twenty-first birthday, just got married, gets out of prison tomorrow, etc.) will die a tragic death before the end of the movie, cradled in the arms of that same character.

SEAN COLLINS

Tyro Transmission Rule. When an inexperienced driver gets behind the wheel for the first time, a special sensor automatically puts the car into reverse gear. This device seems to be a luxury item, since it is often found on expensive cars. It is especially effective near shrubbery, trees, swimming pools, etc.

ADAM SCHINDLER, *Chicago*

Undead Dead

Ultimate B-Western Cliché. It's not "They went that-a-way." It's not "We'll head 'em off at the pass." No, it's "We'll give him a fair trial." (Pause) "And then we'll hang 'em."

MICHAEL SCHLESINGER, Culver City, Calif.

Unattributed Critical Quotation. Words of praise for a film, contained within quotation marks and looking exactly like an excerpt from a review, but with their source curiously missing. There is a reason for that: They do not have a source, but have been written for the occasion by a movie publicist, who hopes that since they look like quotes from real critics, a hasty reader or TV viewer will be fooled.

R. E.

Undead Dead. In horror movies, whenever the killer is killed, he is never dead. This rule is as old as the movies, but was given its modern shape in *Halloween* (1978) when the killer arose from apparent destruction to jump up behind Jamie Lee Curtis. Since then, all of the Dead Teenager Movies, most of the Bond pictures, and many other thrillers have used a false climax, in which the villain is killed–only to spring up for a final threat. In an ordinary thriller, the cliché of the Undead Dead is part of the game–but its use in *Fatal Attraction* was unforgivable.

R. E.

Unheld Peace Rule. The words "speak now, or forever hold your peace" are never used in movie wedding ceremonies unless someone is not going to hold his or her peace.

ALEX TEICH, New York, N.Y.

Universal Movie Computer Operating Laws. (1) All computers in a hi-tech movie have digitized speech and/or a personality. (2) The person typing on a computer speaks aloud what is on the screen, no matter how secret the information is. (3) Every teenage computer user is a hacker and owns a modem (see *WarGames,* etc.). (4) Teenage hackers use computers to pick up girls who don't have a clue about computers.

OLLI LEHTO, *Helsinki, Finland*

Universal Translator. Device carried by all spaceships, allowing instantaneous translation from any alien language into the local language. The most incredible thing about this device is the way it can alter any accompanying visual transmission from the aliens. If you look closely you will see the perfect synchronization of the speaking alien's lips to the lip movements of the local language.

RICHARD ROHRDANZ, *West Kennebunk, Maine*

Unknown Team Member. Used in *Star Trek* movies, cop movies, war movies, etc., whenever a team is on a dangerous mission. The unknown team member, not a recognizable actor, will be dead within forty-five seconds. "Jones is dead, sir" is a standard epitaph.

SAM WAAS, *Houston*

Unmotivated Close-up. A character is given a close-up in a scene where there seems to be no reason for it. This is an infallible tip-off that this character is more significant than at first appears, and is most likely the killer. See the lingering close-up of the undercover KGB agent near the beginning of *The Hunt for Red October.*

STUART CLELAND, *Chicago*

Unselected Short Subjects. Although most sex scenes begin with the characters taking off some of their clothes, there is always a cut before they complete the process, because no male actor can seem sexy while taking off his shorts and socks.

EUGENE ACCARDO, *Brooklyn, N.Y.*

Unsilenced Revolver. Despite dozens of movies which think otherwise, a revolver cannot be silenced, because the sound escapes, not from the barrel where they fit the silencer, but from the gap between the frame and the cylinder. Only closed-breech weapons, like pistols with magazines in the grip, can be silenced—unless you wrap them in a pillow.

DAWSON E. RAMBO, *Las Vegas*

Unsuspecting Students Law. At every high school dance that takes place in the fifties, some ruffian and his greasy-haired friends spike the punch.

RHYS SOUTHAN, *Richardson, Tex.*

Unwise Trust Movie. A new genre in which an unsuspecting baby boomer confides in a psychopathic stranger. Started in recent years by *Fatal Attraction* (casual sex), it has expanded to other areas such as tenants (*Pacific Heights*), baby-sitters (*The Hand That Rocks the Cradle*), roommates (*Single White Female*), policemen (*Unlawful Entry*), and office workers (*The Temp*).

DAVE KALIN, *San Francisco*

Vacuum Sound Effects. Most movies set in space, with the notable exception of *2001, A Space Odyssey,* treat the viewer to a full range of sound effects. Without a medium (air) to transport the sound waves there would, of course, be no sound.

JOHN D. MCCLUSKEY

Vanishing Time Rule. If characters in a movie say they have plenty of time, they will either miss the train/exam/wedding or only get to it by the skin of their teeth.

HILARY POTTS, *West Ealing, London*

V-Barricade. Police cars try to stop getaways by forming a V-shaped barricade that the bad guy can easily bust through. See the end of *Drop Zone,* where the eighteen-wheeler zips through the police obstacle.

GREG BROWN, *Chicago*

Viewable Remains Regulation. Even if a test aircraft plunges 50,000 feet before crashing, the hero pilot lives long enough for the ground crew to pull him free and lie him on the tarmac so he can say good-bye to the heroine. No heroine has yet had to bid a tearful good-bye to a little pool of smoking grease.

RICHARD R. KUNZ, *Chicago*

Vinny Rule. In every movie with Italian-American characters, one must be named Vinny.

DONALD MUNSCH, *Sherman, Tex.*

Visiting Hours Factor. A hospital visit in a movie will *always* end with a nurse informing the characters that visiting hours are over. If the nurse did not appear, the characters would not know when to end the scene and resume the movie.

DAVID FLEISCHER, Toronto

Voice Transplant Syndrome. Aural shock of hearing an actor lip-synching to the voice of a better singer, when you've heard that actor sing in his/her own voice in other movies (e.g., Audrey Hepburn, who warbles in her tolerable mezzo in *Funny Face* and *Breakfast at Tiffany's,* but suddenly becomes a brilliant coloratura in *My Fair Lady,* courtesy of the singing voice of Marnie Nixon).

ANTHONY BRUCE GILPIN, Riverside, Calif.

"Wait Right Here!" Rule. One character, usually male, tells another character, usually female, to "Wait right here. Do *not* follow me into the warehouse, cave, house, etc." The woman inevitably does so, is captured, and must be rescued. Often inspires the line, "I thought I told you to wait outside."

DONNA A. HIGGINS, Prairie du Chien, Wis.

Wash and Wax Rule. In the movies, only the good guys get to drive dirty cars. Any "villain" in a dirty car will be revealed later as having secretly been a good guy.

DON HOWARD, San Jose, Calif.

Watch Your Step Rule. Suicides always choose the ledge with the pigeon.

MATTHEW COPE, Westmont, Quebec

Waterfall Rule

Waterfall Rule. If character falls into a river, it is inevitably just upstream of a major waterfall or series of rapids. This is true no matter how flat the terrain has been to this point or how gentle the stream. No one ever falls into a river downstream from rough water.

JOE DiCOSTANZO, *New York City*

Wayne's World Rule. In any movie based on a television show, at least a quarter of the audience will be involutarily trying to change the channel.

BILL BECWAR, *Wauwatosa, Wis.*

Weak-Ankled Female Syndrome, The. Whenever a man and woman are on the run, the woman inevitably falls and sprains her ankle. As a result, the man must drag or carry her and their progress is slowed, stalled, or halted.

BRIDGETTE CLARK, *Moundsville, W.Va.*

Wedding Cake Rule. In any movie comedy involving a wedding, the cake will be destroyed.

JOHN WECKMUELLER, *Menomonie, Wis.*

We're Alive! Let's Kiss! Inevitable conclusion to any scene in which hero and heroine take cover from danger in each other's arms. (Cf. *High Road to China, Die Hard*—where Bruce Willis kisses his wife, forgetting that he is in a burning building.)

R. E.

Wet Road Rule. Any road seen in a film, no matter how hot or dry the day has been, will be wet, slick, and reflecting headlights after nightfall. This is most commonly seen in deserts and drought-stricken cities like Los Angeles.

EDWARD SAVIO, San Francisco

Wet Star Rule. In Hollywood story conferences, suggested alternative to nude, as in: "If she won't take off her clothes, can we wet her down?" Suggested by Harry Cohn's remark about swimming star Esther Williams: "Dry, she ain't much. Wet, she's a star."

R. E.

"We've Got Company." These words are always used to inform the driver of a vehicle that it is being followed by the police.

R. E.

Wharton's Law. If you were forced to read the book in high school, you'll probably hate the movie too.

ANDY IHNATKO, Westwood, Mass.

What Befits a Legend Least. Any film with the word "legend" in the title won't be legendary. Consider *Legend, The Legend of Billie Jean, The Legend of Lylah Clare, The Legend of Boggy Creek, The Legend of the Lone Ranger, Legends of the Fall, Geronimo: An American Legend, Legend of Tom Dooley, When the Legends Die.* Sole exception: *The Legend of Hell House,* a legendary little thriller.

MERWYN GROTE, St. Louis

What Happened to Our Dreams of Changing the World? A genre first identified by Adam Mars-Jones, in the *London Independent*, 1992. Examples: *Four Corners, Return of the Secaucus Seven, The Big Chill, Indian Summer, Peter's Friends.*

R. E.

"What's That Supposed to Mean?" Dialogue invariably used by accused party in romantic argument. Win bets with your friends while watching made-for-TV melodramas: phrase occurs in every single one.

MICHAEL J. PILLING, *Maple Ridge, B.C., Canada*

Wheels Heels. Movie characters can own rare classic automobiles, but only if they are oblivious to their uniqueness and value, i.e., the Thunderbird in *Thelma and Louise,* the Nash Metropolitan in *The Big Picture,* the Ford Fairlane convertible in *The Adventures of Ford Fairlane,* the old Mercury used as a getaway car in *Thunderbolt and Lightfoot,* the Studebaker Golden Hawk in *The Hot Spot,* the Buick in *Rain Man,* and virtually any pink Cadillac.

MERWYN GROTE, *St. Louis*

Where's Daddy Rule. If two people are having an extramarital affair and one of the partners has a child, the kid will enter the room and ask about the victim parent, to make the lovers feel guilty. See *The Great Gatsby.*

RHYS SOUTHAN, *Richardson, Tex.*

Who Guards the Guards? Anyone who utters the words, "Don't worry—it can't possibly escape!" will be the first to die.

MICHAEL SCHLESINGER, *Culver City, Calif.*

Wild Kingdom Phenomenon. No interesting animal is limited to its natural range. This mismatching probably started with Tarzan films, in which Tarzan rode Asian elephants, fought tigers (Asia only) and cougars (Americas only), wrestled American alligators, and avoided boa constrictors (tropical America only).

STEVE W. ZACK

Willis Duct. In all movies about a lone hero who battles terrorists on a boat/building/plane, there is always one duct which doesn't appear on the terrorists' copy of the blueprints but which the hero immediately locates and uses to escape from the floor/deck/room where the terrorists think the hero is trapped and can do no harm.

ANDY IHNATKO, *Westwood, Mass.*

Windows of the Soul. Any main character who wears glasses will, at least once, take the glasses off to express some deep emotion or give an impassioned speech.

JERRY RITCEY

Women's Battling Backpack Stance. In any fight scene involving a woman and a man, the woman will leap onto the man's back, wrap her legs around his waist, and flail at his head with her pocketbook. The woman is ineffectual and the man lurches around like a bewildered ox. Directors think this is hilarious.

FRANCES PELZMAN LISCIO, *Upper Montclair, N.J.*

Women's Shower Syndrome. Movies with scenes set in women's showers inevitably portray them as brightly lit, open playrooms where nude women laugh, frolic, and snap each other with towels. Those not participating in high jinks are slowly and seductively soaping themselves under the shower spray.

JAMES MOORE, San Jose, Calif.

Wrongheaded Commanding Officer. In modern police movies, the commanding officer exists solely for the purpose of taking the hero off the case, calling him on the carpet, issuing dire warnings, asking him to hand over his badge and gun, etc. (Cf. the Dirty Harry series, *Blue Steel*, etc.)

TONY WHITEHOUSE, Verbier, Switzerland

Wrong Twin Maxim. Whenever there is a chase scene in a crowd of people, the chasers have their hands on the quarry before realizing their captive is not the person they are looking for, but someone who sports the exact same outfit and haircut from the back. That is why it is important for heroes to always shop at popular retail outlets.

BENJAMIN SAGE, New York, N.Y.

Wunza Movie. Any film using a plot which can be summarized by saying "One's a . . ." For example, "One's a cop. One's an actor." Or "One's a saint. One's a sinner."

DAVID KING, Los Angeles

X-Ray Driver. In many thrillers, the hero crashes his car or truck through the window or wall of a building at the precise time and place to allow him to rescue a victim or kill the bad guys. How can he see through the walls to know exactly where his car will emerge? Why doesn't he ever drive into a load-bearing beam?

R. E.

Yakima Canute Rule. Any chase scene involving a fist-fight between the hero and bad guys while they are speeding in a truck or wagon requires the hero to fall over the front of the vehicle, slide between the wheels to the rear, and pull himself up onto the back, surprising the bad guys. (Named after the famous stuntman who originated this move in stagecoach chase scenes.)

SAM WAAS, *Houston*

You Can Go Home Again. In all small-town settings, there is always (a) a parade taking place; (b) a carnival; (c) a shooting gallery, where the girl always outshoots the boy; (d) a picnic basket raffle, always won by the second male and female leads; and (e) a sheriff with the most pronounced accent in town.

MICHAEL KUNKLE, *Santa Rosa, Calif.*

Youngblood Rule. No movie with a hero named "Youngblood" has ever been any good. (Cf. *Youngblood Hawke, Youngblood,* etc.)

R. E.

Your Body Is Waiting. Whenever somebody dies in a hospital, the closest relative or lover finds out by arriving at the hospital and seeing either: (1) orderlies placing a covered body in a waiting hearse or (2) orderlies making the bed of the deceased person. In real life, no covered body is ever loaded into a hearse outside the front door! That's done somewhere out back near the electrical generator.

JIM SIMON, *Villa Park, Calif.*

"You've Got to Believe Me!" Rule. The character who is seeing and hearing things is invariably the only one who knows what is really going on.

BENJAMIN JOHNSON, *Provo, Utah*

Z. Pronounced "zed" in British movies, something most American audiences do not know.

R. E.

Things You Would Never Know without the Movies

I have received the following list from at least a dozen people over the past couple of years. It never comes with an author's name attached. A Web search reveals that it has been reprinted on at least 193 different Web pages, in addition to being forwarded in countless e-mails. It is very funny. Who wrote it? If you did, here's your chance to receive credit for your work. Send me proof of original publication, and I'll add your byline, and send you the special collector's edition of the director's cut of *The Godfather*.

- A cough is usually the sign of a terminal illness.
- A detective can only solve a case once he has been suspended from duty.
- A man will show no pain while taking the most ferocious beating but will wince when a woman tries to clean his wounds.
- A single match will be sufficient to light up a room of any size.
- Action heroes never face charges for manslaughter or criminal damage despite laying entire cities waste by their actions.
- All beds have special L-shaped cover sheets that reach up to the armpit level on a woman but only to waist level on the man lying beside her.

- All computer disks will work in all computers, regardless of software.
- All grocery shopping bags contain at least one stick of french bread.
- All telephone numbers in America begin with the digits 555.
- Although in the twentieth century it is possible to fire weapons at an object out of our visual range, people of the twenty-third century will have lost this technology.
- An electric fence, powerful enough to kill a dinosaur, will cause no lasting damage to an eight-year-old child.
- Any lock can be picked by a credit card or a paper clip in seconds—unless it's the door to a burning building with a child trapped inside.
- Any person waking from a nightmare will sit bolt upright and pant.
- Cars that crash will almost always burst into flames.
- Creepy music coming from a cemetery should always be investigated more closely.
- During all police investigations it will be necessary to visit a strip club at least once.
- Even when driving down a perfectly straight road it is necessary to turn the steering wheel vigorously from left to right every few moments.
- Freelance helicopter pilots are always eager to accept bookings from international terrorist organizations, even though the job will require them to shoot total strangers and will end in their own certain death as the helicopter explodes in a ball of flames.
- Having a job of any kind will make fathers forget their son's eighth birthday.
- Honest and hardworking policemen are traditionally gunned down three days before their retirement.

- If a large pane of glass is visible, someone will be thrown through it before long.
- If being chased through town, you can usually take cover in a passing St. Patrick's Day parade—at any time of the year.
- If being fired at by Germans, hide in a river—or even a bath. German bullets are unable to penetrate water.
- If staying in a haunted house, women should investigate any strange noises in their most revealing underwear.
- If you are blonde and pretty, it is possible to become a world expert in nuclear fission at age twenty-two.
- If you decide to start dancing in the street, everyone you bump into will know all the steps.
- If you find yourself caught up in a situation that could be cleared up quickly with a simple explanation, for goodness sakes keep your mouth shut.
- If you need to reload your gun, you will always have more ammunition—even if you haven't been carrying any before now.
- If your town is threatened by an imminent natural disaster or killer beast, the mayor's first concern will be the tourist trade or his forthcoming art exhibition.
- Interbreeding is genetically possible with any creature from elsewhere in the universe.
- It does not matter if you are heavily outnumbered in a fight involving martial arts—your enemies will wait patiently to attack you one by one by dancing around in a threatening manner until you have knocked out their predecessors.
- It is always possible to park directly outside the building you are visiting.
- It is not necessary to say hello or good-bye when beginning or ending phone conversations.

- It's easy for anyone to land a plane providing there is someone in the control tower to talk you down.
- Kitchens don't have light switches. When entering a kitchen at night, you should open the fridge door and use that light instead.
- Medieval peasants had perfect teeth.
- Most dogs are immortal.
- Most laptop computers are powerful enough to override the communication systems of any invading alien civilization.
- Most people keep a scrapbook of newspaper clippings, especially if any of their family or friends have died in a strange boating accident.
- Mothers routinely cook eggs, bacon, and waffles for their family every morning even though their husband and children never have time to eat it.
- No one involved in a car chase, hijacking, explosion, volcanic eruption, or alien invasion will ever go into shock.
- Once applied, lipstick will never rub off–even while scuba diving.
- One man shooting at twenty men has a better chance of killing them than twenty men firing at one man.
- Police departments give their officers personality tests to make sure they are deliberately assigned a partner who is their total opposite.
- Should you wish to pass yourself off as a German officer, it will not be necessary to speak the language. A German accent will do.
- Television news bulletins usually contain a story that affects you personally at that precise moment.
- The chief of police is always black.
- The chief of police will always suspend his star detective– or give him forty-eight hours to finish the job.

- The Eiffel Tower can be seen from any window in Paris.
- The more a man and a woman hate each other, the more likely they will fall in love.
- The ventilation system of any building is the perfect hiding place. No one will ever think of looking for you in there and you can travel to any other part of the building you want without difficulty.
- Wearing a vest or stripping to the waist can make a man invulnerable to bullets.
- When a person is knocked unconscious by a blow to the head, he or she will never suffer a concussion or brain damage.
- When confronted by an evil international terrorist, sarcasm and wisecracks are your best weapons.
- When driving a car it is normal to look not at the road but at the person sitting beside you or in the backseat for the entire journey.
- When in love, it is customary to burst into song.
- When paying for a taxi, don't look at your wallet as you take out a bill—just grab one at random and hand it over. It will always be the exact fare.
- When they are alone, all foreigners prefer to speak English to each other.
- Word processors never display a cursor on screen but will always say: Enter Password Now.
- You can always find a chainsaw when you need one.
- You can tell if somebody is British because they will be wearing a bow tie.
- You're very likely to survive any battle in any war unless you make the mistake of showing someone a picture of your sweetheart back home.

Mark O'Donnell's Laws of Cartoon Motion

(1) Any body suspended in space will remain in space until made aware of its situation. Daffy Duck steps off a cliff, expecting further pastureland. He loiters in midair, soliloquizing flippantly, until he chances to look down. At this point, the familiar principle of thirty-two feet per second takes over. (2) Any body in motion will tend to remain in motion until solid matter intervenes suddenly. Whether shot from a cannon or in hot pursuit on foot, cartoon characters are so absolute in their momentum that only a telephone pole or an outsize boulder retards their forward motion absolutely. Sir Isaac Newton called this sudden termination of motion the stooge's surcease. (3) Any body passing through solid matter will leave a perforation conforming to its perimeter. Also called the silhouette of passage, this phenomenon is the specialty of victims of directed-pressure explosions and of reckless cowards who are so eager to escape that they exit directly through the wall of a house, leaving a cookie-cutout-perfect hole. The threat of skunks or matrimony often catalyzes this reaction. (4) The time required for an object to fall twenty stories is greater than or equal to the time it takes for whoever knocked it off the ledge to spiral down twenty flights to attempt to capture it unbroken. Such an object is inevitably priceless, the attempt to capture it inevitably unsuccessful. (5) All principles of gravity are negated by fear. Psychic forces are sufficient in most

bodies for a shock to propel them directly away from the earth's surface. A spooky noise or an adversary's signature sound will induce motion upward, usually to the cradle of a chandelier, a treetop, or the crest of a flagpole. The feet of a character who is running or the wheels of a speeding auto need never touch the ground, especially when in flight. (6) As speed increases, objects can be in several places at once. This is particularly true of tooth-and-claw fights, in which a character's head may be glimpsed emerging from the cloud of altercation at several places simultaneously. This effect is common as well among bodies that are spinning or being throttled. A "wacky" character has the option of self-replication only at manic high speeds and may ricochet off walls to achieve the velocity required. (7) Certain bodies can pass through solid walls painted to resemble tunnel entrances; others cannot. This trompe l'oeil inconsistency has baffled generations, but at least it is known that whoever paints an entrance on a wall's surface to trick an opponent will be unable to pursue him into this theoretical space. The painter is flattened against the wall when he attempts to follow into the painting. This is ultimately a problem of art, not of science. (8) Any violent rearrangement of feline matter is impermanent. Cartoon cats possess even more deaths than the traditional nine lives might comfortably afford. They can be decimated, spliced, splayed, accordion-pleated, spindled, or disassembled, but they cannot be destroyed. After a few moments of blinking self-pity, they reinflate, elongate, snap back, or solidify. Corollary: A cat will assume the shape of its container. (9) For every vengeance there is an equal and opposite revengeance. This is the one law of animated cartoon motion that also applies to the physical world at large. For that reason, we need the relief of watching it happen to a duck instead.

MARK O'DONNELL, *New York*

Greg Matty's Creature Ferocity Index

 **T**he Creature Ferocity Index (CFI) can be used by the moviegoer to determine exactly how ferocious the "creature" in a particular movie is supposed to be. The formula is as follows:

$$CFI = NPV + PF + (RL \times 2 \text{ if WAG is yes}) + TDAHDT + SSS$$

Where NPV is the number of potential victims in the movie, one point per PV. For example, the trailer for the movie *Anaconda* appears to have at least six PVs.

Where PF is the pronunciation factor. Score one point for each syllable of the creatures species pronounced differently than we are accustomed to. Using *Anaconda* again, one character pronounces "Anaconda" not as "a–nuh–con–duh," but rather "ahn–uh–cone–duh." In this case, two points are scored.

Where RL is the remote location factor. If the movie takes place in a remote location add a point and if that location is in a foreign country add another. Add a third point if that location is near water and the creature can spend time under water. Here *Anaconda* would score three points.

The RL factor can be multiplied by a factor of two if the local people worship the creature as a god (WAG). *Anaconda* would qualify, upping the RL points to six.

Note that the locals do not count as NPVs unless they are an integral part of the story; see SSS below.

Add a point for each character that mistakenly says something to the effect of, "they don't attack humans do they (TDAHDT)?"

The SSS is the scarred survivor statistic. Add a point for each character that reveals a scar or scars given to him or her by the creature during a prior encounter. Add another point if that character speaks with any kind of foreign accent. This type of character is sometimes a local and because of their SSS status can qualify as a PV.

Based upon the trailer I would estimate *Anaconda*'s CFI to be 18.

$$CFI = 7 + 2 + (3 \times 2) + 1 + 2$$

At my request, Greg Matty applied the CFI to two additional titles, Species *and* Relic.—R. E.

The NPV rating for *Relic* was a little difficult to figure as there were probably 100 or more potential PVs. Then again, half of them were politicians, and they should *never* be considered victims. Also, given the fact that more than one mutilation, mauling, maiming, or murder every ten minutes could place the film in a type of "dead teenager" category, I propose an upper limit of ten to twelve NPVs, depending on the length of the movie. Thus R*elic* would earn around twelve points.

The creature was not a member of an established species so it could not score any PF (pronunciation factor) points. However, its genetic structure brings up the CHGAC variable, which is discussed below.

The RL (remote location) factor was another tough

one as the movie initially took place overseas, then ended up stateside in a museum (of course a museum is probably a very unfamiliar and remote place for some people). Since the beast was worshiped as a god back in its hometown and does spend time under water, I'll let it slide. That yields six points for this area.

No one asked if the creature ever attacked humans since the creature was unprecedented and those who would have been able to give the correct answer were in the process of being consumed anyway. Zero points.

The SSS rating is zero as well, but a sequel poses some interesting possibilities.

Based on this analysis it appears that eighteen total points are to be awarded. This seems relatively low compared to the trailer for *Anaconda*. Although the snake in this movie will no doubt do for the anaconda what Jaws did for the great white shark, I can't help but feel that a genetically altered monstrosity should somehow be more frightening than an ordinary one. Accordingly, I have modified the formula somewhat:

$$CFI = \{NPV + PF + (RL \times 2 \text{ if WAG is yes}) + TDAHDT + SSS\} \times 1.5 \text{ if CHGAC}$$

Where the total points earned are multiplied by 1.5 if the creature has genetically altered characteristics. *Relic*'s final score would be twenty-seven.

$$CFI = \{12 + (3 \times 2) + 0 + 0\} \times 1.5 \quad CFI = 27$$

As for *Species,* the NPV rating is close to *Anaconda* at around eight. PF points are zero for the same reason as *Relic*.

Species takes place in your basic, run-of-the-mill, crime-ridden city so no RL points are awarded. Nor do we know whether "Sill" was worshiped as a god on her home planet. Oh well, no points.

Just as in *Relic,* no points are earned for the TDAHDT factor. Of course in this movie a more appropriate question might have been, "They don't sleep with humans, do they?" No points can be awarded since this question was never asked, although it was answered a couple of times.

In the case of alien movies, I would consider replacing the RL, WAG, TDAHDT, and SSS variables with the DABW phenomenon. Any creature that is disguised as a beautiful woman should be worth at least five points. Especially since we know that sooner or later a male character will be slaughtered while having an intimate encounter with that beautiful woman at the same time her true nature is revealed. A definite five-pointer here for *Species.*

Last, I am pretty certain that the creature was created by splicing human DNA with that of an alien. This would qualify for the CHGAC factor.

This gives a total of twenty points, not bad.

$CFI = (8 + 0 + 5) \times 1.5$ from the modified formula:
$CFI = \{(NPV + PF + (DABW)\} \times 1.5$ if CHGAC

GREG MATTY BOTHELL, *Washington*

A Cynic's Guide to the Language in Film Festival Catalog Descriptions

 Demanding: Unwatchable
Rigorous: Tedious
Playful: Stupid
Unabashed: Shamelessly stupid
Aspires, aims: Fails
Subtle emotions: No acting whatsoever
Beautifully rendered images: Very, very slow
Epic: Very, very long
Provocative: Sex scenes
Daring: Sex scenes with children
Tender: Nudity
Effervescent: Vapid
Ambiguous: Underlit
Gritty: Underexposed
Raucous: Overacted
Outrageous performances: Really badly overacted
Raw: Unedited
Simple story: Underwritten
Fluid camera style: Rock video
Vibrant: At least one nonwhite actor
Urban: All nonwhite actors
Transgressive: All-gay cast
Flamboyant: Transgressive, in drag
Uncompromisingly transgressive: Male-male kissing
Frank: Lesbian cast
Delirious: Amateur
Hybrid: Appeals to fans of neither genre

Majestic: Dull
Mood piece: Plotless
Moody: Suicide-inducing
Sly: Snide
Surreal: Random collection of shots
Uplifting: Naive
Warm, charming: Inane
Heart-wrenching: Sappy
Seamless: Sleep-inducing
Oblique: Opaque
Challenging: Absolutely unwatchable
Intimate: Home movie
Mediatative: Endless
Rich: Overstuffed
Original: Gimmicky
Eerie: Depraved
Unsettling: Nauseating
Understated: No dialogue
Impressive: Director managed to finish it

DOUG SAUNDERS, *Toronto Globe and Mail*